WHAT EVER
HAPPENED TO
COMMITMENT?

What Ever Happened to Commitment?

EDWARD R. DAYTON

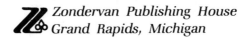

Zondervan Publishing House
Grand Rapids, Michigan

Zondervan Books are published by Zondervan
Publishing House, 1415 Lake Drive, S.E.,
Grand Rapids, Michigan 49506

WHAT EVER HAPPENED TO COMMITMENT
Copyright © 1984 by The Zondervan Corporation

Library of Congress Cataloging in Publication Data
Dayton, Edward R.
What ever happened to commitment?

  Bibliography: p.
  Includes index.
  1. Evangelicalism–United States. 2. Sociology, Christian—United
States. 3. Commitment to the church. 4. United States—Church history.
I. Title.
BR1642.U5D4   1984   280'.4   84-3633
ISBN 0-310-23161-2

Unless otherwise indicated, all Scripture quotations are from the Holy
Bible: New International Version, copyright © 1978 by the International
Bible Society. Used by permission of Zondervan Bible Publishers.

Edited by Julie Ackerman Link
Designed by Ann Cherryman

Printed in the United States of America

84 85 86 87 88 89 / 10 9 8 7 6 5 4 3 2 1

For
Jill,
Patty,
Leigh,
and Rob,
who have life yet to live

Contents

Preface

Every book has something of the life of the author imbedded in it. This one has a lot of mine. It has shaped me, even as I have shaped it. But the shaping has been a process of interacting with people. Sometimes it has been a chance sentence in a conversation. At other times it was long discussions in the night. And then there were those long, hard letters back and forth between me and the editors at Zondervan!

Martin Marty gave me the courage to believe that my analysis of the impact of American culture on American evangelical Christianity was on the right track. Peter Wagner said he liked the second half. Ron Sider thought I could be a lot clearer. My pastor, Paul Cedar, read it and told me where I left him cold and what spoke to him. My small support group had the courage to ask me to review the first draft with them, an experience that convinced me neither I nor the manuscript was ready.

I owe Ken Wilson a special debt. He not only read the third draft and responded with great encouragement, but he proofed it, too! John Iwema, a good brother and former editor at Zondervan, argued with me, coached me, and cajoled me to the point I was ready to forget the whole project. John and I went through three drafts together. Congratulations, John, for your "stick-to-it-iveness." Cheryl Forbes, Zondervan's executive editor of trade books, was the one who convinced me not to quit and who finally showed me the light when it came to leaving out major sections.

The bibliography at the back is a tribute to the many men and women who have enriched my life because they were willing to go through the same long process. It is always upsetting, and sometimes pleasing, to discover that others have thought the same thoughts or felt the same needs. My thanks to many of them and to their publishers for allowing me to quote them.

And then there are all those special people who read and proofed and typed and copied. Carol Kocherhans, Wendy Roan, Diane Tabor, and Susie Payne all deserve particular commendation. And what would I have done without my editor, Julie Ackerman Link?

I am grateful.

In 1831 a young French social scientist by the name of Alexis De Tocqueville visited America. He wanted to understand what America was like, what Americans did, and what they believed. His skills as an observer were exceptional. When he returned to France, he wrote what has become a classic analysis of American life: *Democracy in America*. What he had to say in 1831 may help us better understand where we are today, so we have used quotations from his book to introduce the first twelve chapters of this one.

PART 1

What Ever Happened to Commitment?

CHAPTER 1

What Ever Happened to Commitment?

*The practice which obtains amongst the American, of fixing
the standard of their judgment in themselves alone, leads
them to other habits of mind. They . . . readily conclude that
everything in the world may be explained and nothing in it
transcends the limits of understanding.*   De Tocqueville

Commitment is at the foundation of all human relationships. It is the warp and woof of every society. No matter
where we are in the world, the idea of commitment is well
understood. It may work itself out in different ways, but it
is there. To be human is to long for commitments from
others.

Commitment implies dependability—we sense that we
can count on something or someone. When the world is
falling apart, we trust that someone will be able to put the
pieces back together again. When we hurt and have needs,
someone will come alongside us to help. Commitment
means we can phone a friend at 1:00 A.M., and our friend
will not hang up on us. Commitment means that our
pastor will come when we are sick, that the police will
respond to a scream of terror in the night, that a sleepy
fireman will struggle into his boots and be on the fire
engine within two minutes of the alarm.

At the broader level of society, commitment means that the pieces of green paper in my wallet are worth what the printing on them claims—our government is committed to redeem them at face value. Commitment means someone has taken the responsibility to see to it that water will flow from the faucet when I turn the handle and that lights will brighten the hallway when I throw the switch. Commitment means someone will answer when I dial for the operator.

Commitment is an agreement to work together for the good of a larger group so that each one can have a place and a sense of security. Experience teaches us that traffic signals at street corners enable us to move across a city in a safe and orderly fashion. So we have developed a commitment to traffic laws. Commitment to our society assumes we will act toward one another in ways that are expected and understandable. In Kenya people may think standing in line at a ticket window or at the bank is ridiculous; but in America we are committed to queue, and our sense of rightness is violated when someone tries to shove in front of us.

Commitment to a society or a group is therefore based on the idea that by giving over our allegiance, our time, our feelings about what we would like to do, some larger good will emerge. We assume that if we "do our part," eventually we will benefit. Notice there are two ways of thinking about this: We can make a commitment because we believe it eventually will be for our own good, or we can make a commitment because something in us says this is the "right" thing to do.

Commitment is at the foundation of all human relationships. To put it another way, commitment is what human relationships are all about. For we are made to live in relationship with others. The person who withdraws all commitment to others ceases to be human. Imagine having all the material desires of your heart, but having no one in the world to share them with or no one to admire you for having such fine things. How empty even the most desirable things would be.

Commitment is costly; it always requires giving—our time, our resources, our thought life, even our very soul. And because of its cost we admire it in others and fear it for ourselves. It can hurt. When we give ourselves to others and they turn away from us, revealing that their commitment to us was not as deep as ours to them, we suffer rejection, which can be devastating. When we commit ourselves, we are no longer our own. We give others the right to call on us and even to ask for something we may not be prepared to give.

The ultimate commitment, however, is the one God has made to us, which is evidenced in the life and death of Jesus Christ. In society there are those who may give their life for another who they believe is deserving. But God's commitment to us was so unilateral that He sent His Son to die for us even though there was nothing in us that deserved such a sacrifice.

On the basis of His commitment to us, God calls us to be committed to Him. "You are not your own. You were bought with a price." This is total commitment, for it involves all of life. It is a transfer of allegiance from one kingdom to another. We can say with Paul that "once we were . . . , but now we are. . . ." Total commitment to God, the One who is for us, can be made without fear of rejection, for there is no turning away in His personality. He will never leave us or forsake us.

There is another dimension of Christian commitment, however, that is much harder to accept. Not only are we no longer our own, but we are not just committed to God, either; we are fitted into His body, the church. We are part of one another, and the measure of our commitment to God is our commitment to one another. "All men will know that you are my disciples if you love one another" (John 13:35). We have been called away from our selfish commitments to ourselves and the world to a new commitment to others and to God.

How are we doing?

PROGRESS REPORT

Statistical evidence all around us indicates that this is the day of the evangelical in North America. Between forty and fifty million Americans claim to be "born again." George Gallup's surveys show that the vast majority of Americans hold traditional Christian beliefs about God, Jesus, and the Trinity, the Virgin Birth, Jesus' second coming, and the infallibility of the Bible. Religious bookstores multiply, and books written by Christians or about Christianity are finding their way to best-seller lists. Religious-book publishing houses continue to expand. The range of their output is staggering. A Christian author who once was pleased to sell ten thousand copies of his or her book, may now expect a new book to sell in the hundreds of thousands of copies. Sales of books by religious publishers amounted to almost one billion dollars in 1980.

Evangelical Christians have also taken to the airwaves, broadcasting on nearly 1400 Christian-owned radio stations. Religious TV programs and even religious TV networks are gaining national attention. The PTL Network, which came out of the popular PTL (Praise the Lord) television program, now has almost as many affiliates as the major TV networks. Another network, the Christian Broadcasting Network (CBN), has similar coverage. Both broadcasting networks now have satellite hookups to countries around the world. As one popular book puts it, this is the day of the Super-Church, the Christian Super-Star, and the Christian Super-Athlete.[1]

We even have Christian business directories and Christian Yellow Pages to locate such things as Christian businessmen's committees, Christian women's clubs, and Christian charm schools. Evangelical seminaries abound and prosper. Specialized ministries such as Athletes for Christ, Athletes in Action, and the Fellowship of Christian Athletes are at work. Youth for Christ, Young Life, Inter-

Varsity Christian Fellowship, and Campus Crusade for Christ continue to expand.

A new slogan in the business community is "Jesus Sells." In a *Los Angeles Times* article of November 13, 1980, Doris A. Byron quotes Bill McKay, vice president of Irvine-based American Research Corporation, which commissioned the Gallup Survey, "Without question, there is a Christian market out there. It's a billion-dollar industry."

Liberal forms of Protestant Christianity are in retreat. The mainline denominations, which abandoned evangelism in favor of social concern two decades ago, are now sponsoring major programs of evangelism within their midst. Groups of concerned laypersons multiply: United Presbyterians have their Presbyterians for Biblical Concern; Methodists have a Good News movement; and Lutherans Alert seeks to stimulate the American Lutheran Church. We appear to be in the middle of The Evangelical Renaissance.[2]

BUT SOMETHING IS WRONG

Even in the midst of an evangelical resurgence, however, an uneasy feeling indicates something is wrong. Although the number of Christians multiplies, the depth of their Christianity seems shallow. An overabundance of how-to-do-it books has failed to teach us how to find peace with God, how to have a more satisfying marriage, how to raise a Christian family, how to experience the indwelling of the Holy Spirit, how to have a more fulfilling sex life, how to be a better Bible student, how to do this, how to do that. We have more and more tools to help us find a better Christian life; but strangely, fewer and fewer of us feel at peace. Instead, we get caught up in more and more activities, seeking more and more solutions to life's problems. But the solutions only seem to uncover a wider range of problems. In our quest to keep up with all our activities, we become more and more materialistic, which only adds to our problems. We find that we need all the necessities of the good life to help us keep up our frantic pace—dishwashers because we hardly have time to cook, let alone clean up; automatic garage-door openers because we can't afford to waste the five minutes it takes to get out of the car and raise the door ourselves; hot tubs to soothe our overworked muscles; automatic telephone-answering machines because we are never home to answer it ourselves; and the list goes on. As a result, our constant battles with appliance stores and service agencies to keep our labor-saving devices operating drain away more of our energy than the product could ever conserve. And that "better Christian life" continues to elude us.

As Christians, we believe we are willing to die for our faith, but most of us don't know what we'd die for. If our forefathers "burned out for Christ," we are burning out just trying to keep up with the pace of living. In addition, the variety of religious experience found within the evangelical movement and the resulting wide range of religious practices of local churches confuse us and leave us wondering about the rightness of our own position.

We have a longing for community, but evidently few of us have experienced it. Little of the enthusiasm for communal living generated in the sixties by the Jesus People has carried over to the evangelical community. Yet we yearn to be part of one another, part of something greater than ourselves. But somehow, after the glow of the Sunday morning service, the middle of the week seems sterile of meaningful relationships. We search for community in small groups, but often find it difficult to believe group members really know us, or even want to know us. And perhaps some have already given up their search for meaningful relationships within the body. Statistics show that although the number of those who claim to be born again continues to rise, ten to twenty million of them are not members of a local church. The biblical concept that Christians are all part of one body apparently is outside their understanding. The institutional church is losing its legitimacy.

The electronic church, on the other hand, is booming,

making a joke of God's concept of community. As we sit isolated in our living rooms, watching our TV sets, we feel lonelier and lonelier.[3] The communication skills, the mass-media marketing, and the eye-catching programming that Christians have so easily adopted from the world of commercial television have produced a message with a hollow ring. In our hearts we suspect that just as the hyped-up promises of Crest, Charlie, Chevy, and Chevron will not live up to the glowing claims made by the beautiful people who promote them, neither will the latest brand of commercial Christianity.

MEANWHILE, BACK AT THE WORLD

It is not only our Christian world that is in disarray. Most of us were brought up to believe that the American way of life would not only permeate the world, but that it eventually would bring the world's disasters under control. But now we are not even sure our way of life can survive another generation. Our institutions appear to be out of control, to have taken on a life of their own. "Bureaucracy" is the order of the day. And these bureaucracies are like faceless giants that are controlled by some unseen "they" who carry out their desires in spite of all we do.

So we just watch as the world becomes less and less manageable. Even though evangelicals have been in government, both in the White House and in national legislative bodies, they have been unable to bring about major changes in our government or to find solutions to the problems that plague our nation.[4] Why is a country that produced men like Washington, Jefferson, Franklin, and Lincoln no longer able to find anyone who knows the answers to our country's problems? If "Christ is the answer," why couldn't a born-again Christian president find the answers?

We are surrounded by wars and rumors of wars. The time-honored policy of diplomatic sanctuary was violated when a nation many of us never heard of took Americans captive. We are told that an individual college student can produce an atomic bomb in a homemade laboratory. The world exists under the constant threat of being held hostage by a fanatic who could arm himself with anything from automatic weapons to deadly chemicals.

And because the future is so uncertain, we oscillate between becoming completely engrossed in tomorrow's problems and trying to escape from them by "living only for today." As a result, our economic system has also fallen into disarray. In terms of the future, we wonder, should we save, spend, borrow, or all three? How can we make the future secure? Should we sell mother's silver tea service? Who knows? And suppose we don't have a tea service to sell? On the other hand, we wonder if it's worth the trouble to try to make the future secure. Perhaps there will be no future. Why not just enjoy what we have while we have it? Why wait? Let's buy it now! We need it. We want it. We have to have it.

Our economic insecurities have led to changes in our social priorities. The Flower Children and the Jesus People, so concerned with love, equal rights, and "sharing the wealth" in the sixties, have disappeared. According to a 1980 article in the *Los Angeles Times*, the 1979 annual national survey conducted by UCLA and the American Council on Education showed that nearly two-thirds (62.7%) of 190,151 college freshmen polled said that "being very well off financially" was an important goal. Compared with responses in the late sixties when fewer than fifty percent of those surveyed believed that financial well-being was an important aspiration, this shows a significant trend. Nearly sixty-five percent of college freshmen in 1979 said that an important reason for going to college was "to be able to make more money" later in life. We are no longer as concerned about the needs and rights of our neighbors as we are about our own needs and rights. The Generation of the Flower Children of the sixties that became the "Me Generation" of the seventies has become the "Me Right Now Generation."

All this leaves us with some deep, though often subconscious, questions: Is God really in control? Is there really a God? These questions go much deeper than questions of orthodox belief. They operate at such a profound level that many of us are not even aware of them.

Whatever the future holds, most agree that we are headed for times of tremendous change. Nothing is going to remain the same. For Americans, that may mean we no longer will be able to maintain the standard of living that makes us so different from the rest of the world. Instead of being six percent of the world's population that consumes thirty to forty percent of the world's resources, we may have to become part of the majority. To Christians who have come to equate God's *material* blessings on America with evidence of God's approval, such a future can be frightening.

WHAT EVER HAPPENED TO COMMITMENT?

And so many of us look to the past, to a time when people could be depended on to live up to commitments—when having a commitment was a noble thing in itself—when we could expect a good day's work for a good day's pay. But who believes in that anymore? Every day we encounter people who are more interested in getting in, getting out, getting paid than with how well they do the job. The idea of *service* as a virtue in buying and selling of goods seems to be gone. There was a time when one found satisfaction in knowing there were people who *cared* . The family had time to care. The pastor had time to care. Other Christians within the church had time to care. It was comforting to know there were people who would stop along the roadside to help us change a flat tire or go out of their way to help, just because helping was the right thing to do.

Recently I asked an Indian tailor in Southern Thailand to repair some trousers for me. In my haste to get to my next engagement, I forgot I had left the trousers with him. How surprised I was to receive a phone call in my hotel room 150 miles away. The tailor had tracked me down and was planning to have someone deliver the trousers to me. The cost of the repair was fifty cents.

The world seldom operates like that anymore.

And often, all too often, the church fails to operate like that either. In the nineteenth century era of missions, missionaries sailed for the unknown, well aware that nineteen out of twenty of them would die before returning home. They knew what they were heading into. They took their families with them, knowing that perhaps they would have to bury their children in a strange land. But they were convinced they were going where God had called them to go, and obedience was more important than life itself. Whatever happened to that kind of commitment? Whatever happened to people you could depend upon, organizations you could depend upon? Can we even depend on God anymore?

NOTES

[1]See Jeremy Rifkin and Ted Howard, *The Emerging Order: God in the Age of Scarcity* (New York: Putnam, 1979).

[2]See Donald G. Bloesch, *The Evangelical Renaissance* (Grand Rapids: Eerdmans, 1973).

[3]See Ben Armstrong, *The Electric Church* (Nashville: Nelson, 1979).

[4]Mark Hatfield has spelled out the problem in *Between a Rock and a Hard Place* (Waco: Word, 1977). Perhaps the measures of the Reagan Administration will give us some new encouragement.

[5]"College Freshmen Now Prefer Status and Money, U.S. Survey Discloses," *Los Angeles Times*, January 20, 1980.

CHAPTER 2

Our American World

The more the conditions of men are equalized the more important it is for religion, not needlessly to run counter to the ideas which generally prevail, or to the permanent interests which exist in the mass of the people.

De Tocqueville

The American evangelical church is being overcome by the world. Instead of encouraging a new set of commitments, we, the church, call people to add to their old ones. This is not a conscious apostasy—we do not think of ourselves as "worldly," nor do we have a conscious desire to be conformed to this world. But when the Bible speaks of the "world" and "worldiness," it is speaking of a system that consciously turns itself away from God. And the church in America is guilty of taking on "the American way" without even realizing what it is doing.

An experiment testing a frog's ability to withstand temperature change illustrates what is happening to us. A frog taken from a comfortable water temperature and placed in a bowl of water twenty degrees higher will quickly jump out. The same is true for a ten-degree increase in water temperature. But if the water temperature in the frog's container is raised very gradually, not only will the frog not jump out, he will boil to death.

American culture is doing the same thing to evangelical Christians. As the climate of our culture gradually changes, we adjust to our new environment—and we are not even aware of the change. Nor are we aware that the new environment we have adjusted to is sapping the vitality out of our commitments to one another, our commitments to God, and our commitments to the work to which God has called us.

We have defined "the world" and "worldliness" in such narrow categories (e.g. a list of "don'ts") that we no longer know what the world is. After all, how *does* one tell a Christian from a non-Christian in America? We need to understand the world around us and compare it with biblical norms—what God's Word says the world is supposed to be like. It's a continuing exercise, for the world keeps rewriting the agenda, as well as the rules. The customs and values of America are writing evangelical theology.

Most of these changes happen, however, without our even being aware of them. The culture changes, and we change our theology to fit. For instance, when I was a boy no good Christian woman would be seen in church with her head uncovered. Indeed, in most churches a woman coming to church without wearing a hat would be quickly ostracized. After all, the Bible *is* clear that women should not pray with their heads uncovered. Right? But where are we forty years later? How many churches can we find where women must wear hats or have their heads covered in some way? Very few. What happened? Did some eminent theologian discover that Paul's statement was strictly cultural and then spread the news across the land so that this new doctrine was expounded from hundreds of pulpits? No. Rather, American fashion designers decided women should no longer wear hats, and Christians, being more committed to fashion than to their religious convictions, changed their convictions. This, of course, is not an argument for wearing hats, but it does illustrate how we change our theology to match our culture.

These are strong words—words that should make us very uncomfortable. But we can back them up by exploring our basic American values: what we believe, what we think is important, and how we act toward one another. Sociologists call this "culture." In most of our minds "culture" means the beliefs and practices of the elite. We say, "He is a cultured man." But at a deeper level, "culture" is the system of beliefs and values that dominates the actions of a society. A people's search for the meaning of existence and how the norms, or acceptable average standards, of such a meaningful existence should be enforced are at the core of culture.[1] We want to know who we are, where we fit.

IT'S NOT SOMETHING WE THINK ABOUT

Not many of us think very much about our own culture. We assume that the way we do things and the values we hold are what is good and right and normative to everyday life. Without thinking about it, we assume our values are universal—that right-thinking people everywhere act like we act.

People in most societies act without thinking too much about their actions. Americans are no different. We believe our cultural values, something we sometimes call the American Way, are inherently the best. The belief that America plays a special role among the nations of the world is part of our heritage, part of our history as we understand it. The close correlation between religious and political freedom historically has led us to believe in our Manifest Destiny and to justify our involvement in two world wars because we were "making the world safe for democracy." Our political values are wrapped up in the idea that democracy, and our particular form of it, is the best way to run *any* country.

So how do we begin to understand our own culture? About the only way we can picture it is to contrast it with other cultures. To understand ourselves we have to understand how others see us. This is not easy to do.

Since we believe our way is better, if not the best, we find it convenient to dismiss others' judgments of us. And for Americans it is especially difficult, since it is part of our culture to assume, when two things are different, that one must be better than the other. The Chinese, on the other hand, may view American culture and say, "That's the American way, and this is the Chinese way," without implying one is better than the other. But Americans will invariably say, "The American way is better than the Chinese way." Or, as some Americans have admitted lately, "Perhaps the Chinese way is better." This phrasing, however, still implies one is better than the other.

As Christians we understand that we are to stand firm against the influences of the world. Every church and every new Christian face this crisis of changing their commitment from the world to God. A new landscape must be learned, new directions found. We are citizens of a new government and a new kingdom, even while we maintain our life in our former one.

But each society is different, and as the gospel comes to each one, different changes must take place among those who declare themselves to be the body of Christ. Some cultural values and practices are obviously anti-biblical, and thus anti-Christian. Early missionaries to the South Pacific Islands encountered a culture in which the people felt the best way to handle the problem of what to do with a dead man's wife was to strangle her. The missionaries insisted such a practice could not continue; and they were right.

Other values are neutral or can be adapted into Christian practice. The Christmas tree most of us have in our homes each year was once the symbol of Nordic gods. But as a symbol it is harmless, now that its meaning has been transferred to a Christian celebration.

On the other hand, many non-Christian societies have values that are very Christian. For instance, societies that place a high value on family responsibility and allegiance obviously fit well into biblical teaching.

THE CHRISTIAN EDGE

But as American Christians we have an advantage. As the gospel has spread to all the nations of the world, we have seen God's grace extended to men and women in thousands of different cultures. The Word broke into history and was found "among men" within a culture. If we travel to the different continents of the world, we will find Christians who have all the marks of what we call evangelicalism, but who think quite differently than we do about many things. The fact that God accepts them *within their culture* in the same way He accepts us within our culture, encourages us to look at ourselves, not with the idea that we are necessarily better or worse, but different.

This is an important point. If God is willing to establish His Church in cultures dramatically different from our own, cultures whose value systems are often at right angles with our American values, then this must give us pause. If we were only talking about differences in doctrine, that would be one thing. But throughout the world we find hundreds of thousands of men and women we would have to identify as being saved, born again, and walking with Christ, who often have values quite different from our own. Indeed, *they* cannot understand how we, American evangelicals, can call ourselves Christians and do some of the things we do. But rather than be discouraged by these differences, let us believe they have something to teach us as we examine American culture and its impact on our churches.

AMERICANS ARE DIFFERENT

Against almost any cultural continuum, Americans will be found at one end, not because all other cultures are very much alike, but because ours is different. Every culture is a mosaic of values and norms. But when we examine these values and norms one by one, Americans are often at the extreme end of many of them.

This should not surprise us. The forces at work in the

world when the U.S. was founded were unlike those of any other period in history. Not only is the U.S. a relatively new country among the nations of the world, but it is the only major country founded on the basis of a Protestant Christian ethic.

This last difference has led many to believe that Christianity and American culture are one and the same. Consequently, when American cultural values began to deteriorate, so did our Christian religious values. Like the frog in the pot of gradually warming water, the church never noticed the change and, without questioning, changed its values as its cultural environment changed.

NOTES

[1]For a discussion of the concept of culture as one of a trinity of social dimensions, see Daniel Bell, *The Cultural Contradictions of Capitalism* (New York: Basic, 1976). The other two elements of this trinity are religion and economics. Bell argues that we first lost religion and now economic control.

CHAPTER 3

How Americans Think

Those who cultivate the sciences mistrust systems; they adhere closely to facts, and study facts with their own senses.

De Tocqueville

All societies assume that every other society uses the same thinking process. This idea is so firmly imbedded within us that it is difficult even to talk about it. After all, if I cannot think the way you do, how can I understand how you think?

Perhaps the differences can be best understood by comparing literate and non-literate societies. Literate societies, those that have learned to reduce ideas to written form, are forced to express those ideas in logical sequence because the very act of writing things down requires a sequential way of thinking. Sentence A is followed by sentence B which is followed by sentence C.

To put it another way, writing things down explains the way we think, even as it shapes the *way* we think. Not many years ago the phrase "woman's intuition" was freely used in American society to describe the phenomenon that somehow someone had come to the correct conclusion without being able to explain the process used to reach that conclusion. The assumption was (and is) that right thinking, rational thinking, must be verbally explainable. But, as we now well know, the mind is not restricted to "linear" thinking, nor is *how* we reach conclusions so easily described.

For a decade or so we used the electronic computer as a possible model for the mind. We now see that the human mind is far more complex, far more adaptive and creative, than we are even able to imagine.[1] For example, many Africans learn to think in "circular" patterns and arrive at valid conclusions in ways entirely different from ways used in the West. This phenomenon is much more apparent to those living outside a Western context than it is to us. I well remember sitting up late one evening with a Kenyan brother discussing the pros and cons of his completing his education in an American university. He was concerned that he would lose his ability to think like an African.

American thinking patterns lie somewhere between theoretical speculation and empirical description.[2] Whether or not an idea has any value is based on whether or not it has any application. According to Daniel J. Boorstin, "Americans . . . have discarded the European tradition of evaluating ideas or systems of thought according to . . . 'aesthetic appeal.' "[3] In fact, Americans are very suspicious of those who emphasize such aesthetic values. This is not to say that we have no aesthetic sense. Some studies show that a great deal of "scientific" thought is dominated by the aesthetic—for example, the search for symmetry. But generally, Americans do not like to be *thought of* as being aesthetic, of putting *value* on the beautiful, the lovely, or that which is pleasing to some ill-defined and thus "unscientific" inner self.

Americans have a great ability to think in abstract terms. We talk about "models" and "analogies" and "systems" as though they were reality, rather than an attempt to express reality. Such models of thinking permit us to talk about all kinds of things without really describing anything. Many cultures, on the other hand, communicate in terms of descriptions or stories about life. When we listen to an African or a Chinese tell story after story, we ask ourselves, "When will he get to the point?" What we don't realize is that the sum of the stories *is* the point.

One result of our abstract thinking, though, is reductionism in much of our theology. We want to "boil things down" to a final conclusion. Consequently, our theology is often a list of concepts or notions that the average lay person has little ability to tie into everyday living.

HOW EVANGELICALS THINK

We should not be surprised to discover that middle-class American evangelicals think the same way as most middle-class Americans. The difficulty is that we often do not distinguish between biblical thinking and American thinking. We, like all cultures, have built-in biases that color the world around us. An obvious example of our failure to recognize these biases is how we apply Western thinking and logic to the writings of the Bible, particularly the Old Testament.

God's Word was initially given to a people who had quite a different thinking process than the one most of us in the West now use. If we are to understand what God was attempting to say to the Hebrews, as well as to the Christians to whom the Bible is addressed, we must get beyond the words. After all, if God's Word is intended for all people and all cultures, then somehow each culture must attempt to understand what this Word means to its own culture in its particular place and during a particular time. Christians in a number of other cultures seem to understand this intuitively. Unfortunately, it is far from the understanding of most American evangelicals. We want to take verse and chapter and make direct application without understanding the larger context.[4]

When it comes to our understanding of the church, we can go from one extreme to the other. We can either assume that the biblical writers had our same thinking process—A, B, C, and then D—and conclude that our churches should be exactly as churches were nineteen hundred years ago, or, on the other hand, we can use "rational thinking" to conclude that that day was completely different from our own. This "rational thinking," however, can cause all kinds of problems for Christians. It can rob us of the mystery of God's Word as we attempt to explain everything in neat packages. It can make us critical of the inner light that may be flickering in someone else's life. It can take away the joy of just accepting God at His word. And it can separate us from other local fellowships that have worked things out differently.

A part of Christian maturity is the ability to hold on to the rational and yet allow the mystery, the paradox. There is a longing in all Americans for *answers*, to know something is either right or wrong. Both the extreme left and the extreme right in America stem from the mindset that two apparently different conclusions cannot both be right. The evangelical "right" appears to come out of this same tension.

FACTS ARE FACTS, AREN'T THEY?

The American world is full of facts. We reason by beginning with what we consider facts, and then we proceed to ideas. We assume that some things "are," while others are speculative. In other words, we generally think inductively, from what "is" to what "can be." Americans are pragmatists, but it is our incessant need to put the world in order, to "sort out the facts," that makes American thinking unusual. This style of thinking leads us to emphasize consequences and results. "How will what I am about to do affect my world?" Unlike many Europeans who want to begin with the reality of ideas and theories, the American first wants to judge the worth of such things. Americans therefore stress method-proven ways of doing things.

The time and motion studies that multiplied the effectiveness of American industry at the turn of the century all began with facts. The father of modern time and motion study, Frederick Taylor, wanted to know what was the most efficient way for one man to shovel a ton of coal. What was the best angle for a cutting tool in making a locomotive wheel? What was the fastest way to move an object from point A to B with the least amount of energy? Americans like to break things down into subdivisions and analyze each as a separate entity. This inductive style of thinking is in contrast to relational styles of other cultures in which individual parts are seen as part of a whole, with every part (and every person) somehow related to another part. In this relational style of thinking, personal experiences are given value equal to empirical facts.

People in other societies often equate experience, or feelings, with facts. They consider what they feel to be as important as what they *know*. Americans cannot understand this. While many other societies view "data" as only part of reality, we demand "hard evidence" and an ability to repeat a scientific experiment.

AN EVANGELICAL RESPONSE

American evangelicals take as their foundation the notion that what they *believe*, not what they do, is of utmost importance. For many of us, our faith has thus become a series of propositions—statements that are either right or wrong, but totally separate from what we do. This permits us to eat our cake and have it too. We can enjoy the benefits of our secular culture while still holding on to our carefully constructed belief system, seldom allowing the two to interfere with one another. And so we isolate what we believe from what we do; we divide fact from all responsibility for those facts; and we are left with "truth without consequences."

Propositional faith focuses on "right belief" and originates from our emphasis on "only believe." It fails, however, to focus on the consequences of what it is we believe. For example, it permits us to center our beliefs in a certain set of historical facts, such as those Paul gave us in his propositional definition of the gospel in 1 Corinthians 15, but to ignore the consequences inherent in those facts and in that belief. This is the kind of "wisdom" the same apostle railed against in the first chapter of 1 Corinthians. James called this kind of wisdom "earthly, unspiritual, of the devil" in James 3:15 and contrasted it with heavenly wisdom in the same chapter, verses 17–18: "But the wisdom that comes from heaven is first of all pure; then peace loving, considerate, submissive, full of mercy and good fruit, impartial and sincere. Peace-makers who sow in peace raise a harvest of righteousness."

Notice the *actions* associated with wisdom. There must be a connection between what we believe and what we do. Biblical wisdom acts. Truth *has* consequences.

The Bible identifies belief, or faith, as a beginning point and shows little tolerance for the American "either-or" mentality that allows for no middle ground. Men and women are called out of darkness into light, from being slaves to Christ. Our status changes immediately, but our journey has just begun. Too often the missionary efforts of the American church have failed at this point. In a desire to bring people to right belief, we have often taught them something quite foreign to their culture—namely, that belief can be separated from action. We have neglected to talk about the demands the gospel places on both the gospel proclaimer and on those being called to Christ.

Our response in the local church has been similar. "Only believe" is cheap grace. It demands no commitment. It assumes that if we believe right, we (as individuals) are all right. As a result, we have Lone Ranger Christians outside the fellowship of a local church as well as people who are filling congregations but who are not taking responsibility for the community into which they have been called. This lack of commitment to one another makes it easy for believers to shade a business deal a little, to give in to the pressures of the world, but still to be pleased with the pastor's sermon on Sunday.

CAUSE AND EFFECT

Just as Americans tend to subdivide and analyze, we also have a profound belief that every happening is a result of something that happened prior to it. There is always cause and effect. "The idea of a natural 'happening' or 'occurrence' is not a familiar or acceptable one for Americans, as it is for instance for the Chinese. Americans are not satisfied with statements of fact until they have determined who is responsible—who did or who caused it to be done. 'Where there's smoke, there's fire' means that each effect or event has a causative agent."[5]

Other cultures do not have this strong sense of cause and effect. For example, if a maid in a Latin American home knocks the dishes off the table as she brushes by them, when asked what happened, she will reply, "The dishes fell off the table." She feels little need to find an immediate cause. She only states what happened. (She is not ignorant of the fact that she knocked the dishes off the table, but she fits the event into a much larger and undefinable worldview.) Americans do not know what to do with this kind of view of the world. We are conditioned to look for the immediate cause.

A friend of mine who was attempting to train electronic technicians in a Latin American country found his situation incomprehensible. When the people he was attempting to train made a mistake, they refused to accept that they were the *cause*. They did not perceive *themselves* as making the mistake. They saw no need to connect the event with themselves. When I used the example of the maid to illustrate the difference in Latin American and American thinking, my friend responded, "That's right! They refuse to admit it! They are liars!"

AN EVANGELICAL RESPONSE

Note the relationship between evangelical fact-centeredness and the American penchant for determining a cause for every effect. In such a culture facts are important.

The current dispute over the so-called "inerrancy" of the Bible has an obvious made-in-America ring to it. Even the "solution" to the problem (that the text of the Bible has within it apparent "technical" self-contradictions) is an appeal to the original *cause:* namely, that in the "original text," Scripture was without error.[6]

We fail to see how uniquely American is this intense drive to *prove* that the Bible is *scientifically* all right. We appeal to our understanding of science to judge the Bible, and in so doing we place a *scientific* understanding above the revealed Word. One wonders how the Holy Spirit managed to spread the gospel before the Age of Science!

To make matters worse, we attempt to export our own understanding of the way the world works, often with disastrous results. Time and time again I hear brothers and sisters from churches in other countries plead that we not export our American problems. But how arrogant we are! How unwilling we are to believe that the Holy Spirit may have taught Christians in some "foreign land" things we ourselves were unable to hear.

The American emphasis is on what is pragmatic, what works. Americans do not like to work within theoretical frameworks. Thus we find the average evangelical studying or memorizing the Scripture text, rather than the total meaning of Scripture. We are satisfied with "knowing the Bible," rather than understanding and doing what the Bible says. Obviously, there is nothing wrong with studying and memorizing specific texts. But as Christians in other cultures may be seeking to understand what God is trying to communicate, we American evangelicals too often want to come to agreement with one another on what the Bible *says*. We have a tacit, underlying assumption that "what it says" is a given, and that once we discover what it says, that knowledge can be held as a fixed fact for future reference.

Too often the result is a division between preaching the gospel and living the gospel. Rather than analyze the *implications* of the gospel as Jesus gave them, we would much rather focus on ourselves, on the individual: "What must *I* do to be saved?"

The American desire for formulas and solutions to problems is typified by the popularity of the Institute in Basic Youth Conflicts seminar led by Bill Gothard. These thirty-two-hour, six-day seminars have often drawn five to ten thousand people, even when presented on video. "Alumni" are permitted to return again and again free of charge to make sure they have absorbed all the principles. Here, neatly packaged in a large, red notebook, are the answers to the vast majority of life's problems. Note the "interchangeable parts" aspect of all of this. (More about that later.) Gothard assumes that people's lives and problems are so similar that the solutions also can be similar. American evangelicals like to believe that God has a set of principles that form the basis of right living for anyone. (I remember how shocked I was when a publisher put "God's Principles for Christian Organizations" on the back jacket of a book Ted Engstrom and I had written. The publisher may have believed we had found some of God's principles, but Ted and I were never aware that we had!)

But even here, in solutions such as those packaged in Gothard's notes, we find little emphasis on how we should reach out to the rest of the world. The focus is on the individual and the individual's actions in *response* to the world. There is little consciousness that the Bible has charged the *church* to do the work of Christ throughout the world, that we are to proclaim the advent of His Kingdom in both word and deed. It focuses on me, and on my need.

As another example, note the underlying assumption of the "Four Spiritual Laws" approach as it was initially used by Campus Crusade for Christ. We are told that these "laws" have been widely tested as a means of evangelism. We are further told that approximately ten percent of the people with whom these laws are "shared" pray a prayer of faith to receive Christ. What is not clear is why ninety percent fail to respond. Most explanations center on either the failure of the person who was sharing the laws or the "hardening of the heart" of the person with whom they were shared. But is not this just another example of the American desire to have a formula, of coming up with a solution and then looking for a problem?

The intrinsic belief in solutions and formulas, along with the American world view that sees the world as problems to be solved, makes most evangelicals quite uncomfortable with the paradoxes of the Bible. As a prominent evangelical theologian told me recently, "I have no patience with paradox in the Bible. Christian belief is rational belief." And yet, beginning with the problem of evil in the world and who is responsible for it, to the question of the sovereignty of God versus the freedom of people, the Bible presents a series of paradoxes (*apparent* contradictions) to us. How easily we forget the doctrine of the (partial) imcomprehensibility of God. For the day that we are able to say "I completely understand," we have reasoned away our Creator. Americans and American evangelicals are very uncomfortable with anything that is even partially incomprehensible. We need to *understand.* And in our very assumption that we *can* understand we draw boundaries around God, or, to use J.B. Phillips' phrase, "We put God in a box."

Our constant concern for answered prayer is another example of our cause and effect thinking processes. The Bible often says that God answers prayer. So when we pray and our prayers are not answered according to our expectations, we are compelled to find the reason. Did we pray without believing? Were we double-minded? Did we ask for wrong things? Why? What was the *cause*? In extreme cases, we even become demanding. "Hey, God, You are supposed to give me a reason!" And Paul's response to such a hasty reaction does not make us very happy. "But who are you, O man, to talk back to God? Shall what is formed say to him who formed it, 'Why did you make me like this?'" (Rom. 9:20).

LEGALISM OR LICENSE

The response of evangelicals to American culture appears to go in two directions at the same time. Those who emphasize what a person believes place an emphasis on formulas, which can easily lead to legalism. Others, who share the American desire to "get in touch with themselves," emphasize feelings and experience, which can just as easily lead to license. Both legalism and license are a response to American culture.

Evangelicals who establish their own set of standards as to what is right and what is wrong retreat into a Christian fortress mentality, wanting nothing to do with "worldly Christians." Such legalism easily leads to an unfeeling self-righteousness: "After all, facts are facts." Local churches that emphasize the how-to-do-it approach to Christian experience are typified by an emphasis on a great deal of Bible study, usually taught by an authority figure who is willing to be quite specific about what is right and what is wrong. This approach to religion makes it very easy for such Christians to identify with the political right. The coalition of right-wing evangelicals that began to form as a political entity during 1979 is very much a response to this mixture of American culture and American evangelicalism.

JUDGE ONE THING BY ANOTHER

Cause and effect is related to another cultural pattern: judging one thing by another. Cause and effect sees things in relationship, in a series, and makes it difficult for us to see something standing alone. "The American resists describing or judging something in terms of itself or in its own context. Instead, he insists on a comparison. He evaluates himself against others like himself; . . . he judges his children against the norm for their age; and then, most naturally, he judges other people against Americans. The evaluation of 'good because' is more naturally rendered as 'good as.'"[7]

Notice how this helps us avoid appeals to intrinsic

values or standards. By comparing the thing to be evaluated with other similar things, we permit the individual to make a choice on the basis of personal preference. Most Americans do not realize that we tend to formulate problems, seek solutions, and make choices most readily when we can compare things on the basis of economics or on the basis of technology. We see the result of this in the American management style. How often have I heard myself say, "Don't give me a choice of one. Give me options I can compare." There is nothing wrong with comparing things as such. It is only when we avoid seeking the *absolute* standard that comparing causes us difficulty. How great the temptation to think, and sometimes even say, "Well, I'm certainly better than *most* people!"

AN EVANGELICAL RESPONSE

Even while insisting that every individual is a unique personality, American evangelicals refuse to accept uniqueness. Like other Americans we have a basic need to compare. We want to know how this week's Sunday school attendance compares to last week's. We want to know whether church A is growing faster than church B. When we discover that the church which apparently has deep biblical commitment and biblical concern for the world is not growing, we wonder how this can be. We assume that growth, be it in numbers of people, in physical plant, or in finances, is indeed a testimony to God's blessing.

Quantity often becomes our measure of "God's blessing" on the individual or the organization. How often have we heard, "If God is in it, it will grow"? By definition, then, any Christian enterprise that grows must have "God in it." And yet we have seen organization after organization that has prospered, apparently under the hand of God, only to desert its evangelical roots. Some of the major colleges and universities of our country, such as Harvard and Yale, began as evangelical Christian schools but now deny many of the beliefs on which they were founded.

At the same time we overlook (or don't like to discuss)

the opposite side of the coin: if it is not growing, evidently God is not in it. We do not know what to do with a church like the Church of the Savior in Washington, D.C., which has had broad impact on the Washington community, but which, in actual membership, is not very large.[8]

We carry this same comparison into our individual lives. We either assume that anything we can do, others can do, or that something someone else can do, we should be able to do. Peter Wagner has called the former "gift projection."[9] Since we fail to see that God bestows gifts in different ways, we assume that any gift we have, such as the gift of evangelism, everyone else should have too.

Again we deny the very uniqueness that we claim for the individual. If, instead of comparing individuals, we would ask where each individual fits in the body of Christ, the need to compare would disappear. Wagner helps us understand that we are individually gifted, *but gifted for the service of the church*. This is an important idea that evangelicals need to grasp.

"Judge not, lest you be judged" well sums up our need to be free of comparing. For if I am consistently judging other parts of Christ's body, am I not really criticizing myself, and is not the entire body therefore weakened?

THE WORLD IS A BIG MACHINE

The American belief in cause and effect fits in with the American view that the world is rational, machinelike. Events can be explained. We can determine the reason certain things occurred. We assume the world is mechanistic and material. The sun will come up tomorrow. The law of gravity will still apply. We may not be able to control earthquakes today, but someday we will understand how they "work," and we will be able to take appropriate action.

Ultimately, a mechanistic world is a materialistic world. A world that is nothing more than a huge machine is a world that can be "fixed" when it's not working properly. And what does it take to fix most broken-down machines?

Money. Careful financing. Responsible budgeting. And so we proceed to look for ways to find more money to "fix" our social-economic-political machine.

The idea of a mechanistic world also causes us to assume that machines are perfect and that only humans "make errors." Early in my life I worked for a company that designed flight instruments for aircraft. Every time there was an aircraft accident, our first concern was, "Was it caused by one of *our* instruments?" If the accident had been caused by instrument error, we would have felt personally responsible because of our belief that machines make no mistakes. The instrument could not have malfunctioned unless the people who designed it had failed. How relieved we were to hear that the accident was caused by "pilot error." Someone other than us—in this case the pilot—had failed. There was never any thought given to the possibility that the instrument itself was totally to blame.

AN EVANGELICAL RESPONSE

Most American evangelicals would probably deny that they believe in a mechanistic and material world. After all, do we not believe in the existence and power of the Holy Spirit? But where is any evangelical objection when this view is taught every day in our public schools? Oh, we want to fight for a creationist view of the origin of the universe, but we unthinkingly buy into and even applaud the scientific approach to solving the world's problems. A mechanistic ("scientific") view makes people nothing more than interchangeable parts. It assumes that what cannot be "scientifically" demonstrated cannot be utilized. It finds no place for prayer, no place for higher spiritual values.[10]

Few Christians think through the ultimate consequences of a mechanistic view of the world. For if the world is a big machine, it can be adjusted like any other machine. But most of the world's major problems are *people* problems—social problems. They are the result of humankind dealing with humankind. War is a people

problem. Poverty is a people problem. And people problems cannot be solved scientifically the same way we solve
mechanical problems, unless we are willing to admit that
human beings are just as expendable as worn-out parts—
when they no longer work and cannot be fixed, we replace
them. According to this philosophy, our lives are determined by "a higher good"—our value to society. If we
believe that, then the only "solution" lies in B. F. Skinner's
philosophy that we must move "beyond freedom and
dignity" to a benevolent society that controls all thought
and action.[11]

Christianity conflicts with this mechanistic view of the
world by teaching that humankind's sin—not humankind
itself—is the fundamental problem of the world and that
the only cure for sin is a change in values—not to any
values, but to God's values. More "things" won't change
our fundamental nature, nor will better health, better food,
cleaner water, or better education change our values. Only
conversion, a turning away from sin to God through Christ,
will change our natural, selfish inclinations. As we noted
earlier, we need to turn from sin, come out of the world,
and embrace this new set of values that will cause us to
develop relationships in which we genuinely care for one
another.

THE GREAT GOD TECHNOLOGY

On one hand, we have an apparent national loss of
confidence in ourselves as a nation. On the other hand,
Americans have an innate belief in the power of technological solutions. And evangelicals support this belief,
almost to the point of abandoning the God of people for
the God of technology. Recall the large number of Americans in the early 1980s who were unconvinced there really
was an oil shortage. They apparently did not believe
government officals in Washington, but were willing to
believe that America's scientists could come up with a
substitute for oil. This belief in technology extends to
many dimensions of the Christian life. Perhaps the most

obvious, and at the same time notorious, is what I would call "Technological Evangelism." Ironically, Christians who claim to believe every individual is unique (e.g., "God has a wonderful plan for your life") at the same time seem to believe God wants to deal with all these unique individuals with assembly-line principles. Thus we talk about "means and methods" of evangelism, and although it is seldom stated directly, our home-training programs and our step-by-step methodologies imply that if we just get the method right, results are assured. If people do not respond to our "proven" methods, we automatically assume their hearts are hardened. This is not a recent phenomenon. The famous nineteenth-century evangelist Charles Finney was also convinced that the proper use of methods would always result in conversion.

Our belief in methods leads us to a very precarious position: while claiming to believe in the uniqueness of the individual, we deny that God may have a unique strategy for wooing that individual to Himself. We have allowed means and methods to become our driving force. The individual is nothing more than a part of a (technological) system.[12] We have become separated from the real world by a layer of technology that completely isolates us. Reality is covered over by artificial experience. We have become observers rather than participants in the world. Somehow, that which is real is always just beyond our grasp.[13]

This belief in methods has its impact on every dimension of life. The answer to every problem is a search for another "solution." Instead of listening to one another and feeling with one another, we set about to solve one another's problems.

As one wise man has said, most of life's problems have to be *lived.* And it's in the living that we discover the God of all creation who feels and cares and loves us and plans nothing but the best for us.

NOTES

[1]More recent models of the brain picture it as something like the flora and fauna at the bottom of the ocean, which move and touch and interact randomly.

[2]For a discussion of the concept of culture as one of a trinity of social dimensions, see Daniel Bell, *The Cultural Contradictions of Capitalism* (New York: Basic, 1976). The other two elements of this trinity are religion and economics. Bell argues that we first lost religion and now economic control.

[3]Edward C. Stewart, *American Cultural Patterns: A Cross-Cultural Perspective* (LaGrange Park: Intercultural Press, 1972), 22.

[4]The power of God's Word is often rediscovered by studying a complete book of the Bible that has been typeset without verses, paragraphs, or chapter numbers. This "manuscript method," which was first pioneered by Paul Singer of Inter-Varsity, forces us to look at what the Bible really *says*.

[5]Stewart, *American Cultural Patterns*, 28.

[6]The inerrancy argument has been brought to the fore by Harold Lindsell in his book *The Battle for the Bible*. But as Robert Webber points out, the urgent need in the inerrancy crisis is not to create new schisms but to recover the basis of authority as understood by the early church.

[7]Stewart, *American Cultural Patterns*, 29.

[8]For more on the Church of the Savior, see Elizabeth O'Connor, *The New Community* (New York: Harper and Row, 1976).

[9]C. Peter Wagner, *Your Spiritual Gifts Can Help Your Church Grow* (Glendale: Regal, 1979).

[10]The trend of the last decade to once again teach values in American public schools is to be applauded. Unfortunately, the many texts on value clarification assume that the important thing is not to discover values that are right for everyone, but only to clarify one's own values.

[11]See B. F. Skinner, *Beyond Freedom and Dignity* (New York: Bantam, 1972).

[12]For a broader discussion of the implications of this view and suggested ways of dealing with it, see Edward R. Dayton and David A. Fraser, *Planning Strategies for World Evangelization* (Grand Rapids: Eerdmans, 1979).

[13]Jacques Ellul describes this phenomenon in *Technological Society* (New York: Random House, 1967). For an excellent discussion of the role of television in separating us from reality, see Jerry Mander, *Four Reasons for the Elimination of Television* (New York: Morrow, 1977).

CHAPTER 4

I Am Me!

The citizen of the United States is taught from infancy to rely on his own exertions in order to resist the evils and difficulties of life. De Tocqueville

Some years ago an article in *Reader's Digest* told about an anthropologist who was the first Westerner to visit a remote village. He reported that the people of the village had absolutely no concept of themselves as individuals. They all saw themselves as part of a larger whole, a larger "self." Only after the visiting anthropologist took photographs of them and made recordings of their individual voices did they begin to see themselves as individuals. Then, for the first time, they began to deal with one another as individuals. The anthropologist's plea to the outside world was that we not contaminate such societies with our Western views of individualism.

SELF-CENTEREDNESS

The American concept of decision-making illustrates how individualistic our culture actually is.

From the earliest age, the American child is encouraged to decide for himself—to make up his own mind; he is encouraged to believe he himself is the best judge of what he wants and what he should do. Even in those instances where the American cannot decide for himself, he still prizes the illusion that he is the locus of decision-making. Thus, when he needs to consult a banker, teacher, counselor or expert of any kind, he perceives it as seeking information and advice that helps him to make up his own mind. The expert is treated as a resource person and not as a decision-maker. The American believes, ideally, that he should be his own source of information and opinions and, also, solve his own problems. Esthetic judgments are frequently equated with personal preferences, since the American often resents accepting canons for judging the worth of a work of art. He prefers that value reside in the self; if the individual likes it, it is good. *The result is an intense self-centeredness of the individual* [italics mine]—so striking that an American psychologist has suggested this as a universal value.[1]

The American concept of decision-making contrasts with that of many other cultures. Majority rule is not always considered the best alternative, and people in other cultures often believe that someone other than the individual involved can sometimes make better decisions for that individual. For example, in many societies parents still choose their child's future husband or wife. They assume that since they raised the child they have a better understanding of the kind of mate best suited for him or her. Further, in Japan the majority will almost always respect the rights of a minority and consequently seek a consensus opinion.

AN EVANGELICAL RESPONSE

Evangelical Christianity centers on *personal* belief and experience, basically stating, "You can do it. If *you* (as an individual) will believe, then *you* (as an individual) can be all that you can and should be." Lest I be misunderstood, let me emphasize the importance of coming to Christ one by one. Ultimately the mark of our citizenship in the kingdom is the indwelling of the Holy Spirit. The Holy

Spirit does not indwell an amorphous community. But the important thing is that individuals *are* part of a community. And being part of community is no easy task. It is much easier to ignore the truth that when we became Christians, we became "stuck" with one another.

Robert Webber says it well. "Christianity is not 'my experience' with Christ, as important as that may be, rightly understood. Rather, Christianity is the objective event of God incarnate in Jesus Christ who died and was raised again to establish a new humanity, the church. It is in and through the church as Christ's body that the experience of Christianity is realized."[2]

God calls us out of the world one by one. But what so many evangelicals have missed is that He also calls us *into community*, a community where the first thing we are to put aside is our individualism. "Now you are the body of Christ, and each one of you is a part of it" (1 Cor. 12:27). God has gifted us, not for individual work, but for the work of this particular body. "It was he who gave some to be apostles, some to be prophets, some to be evangelists, and some to be pastors and teachers, to prepare God's people for works of service, *so that the body of Christ may be built up* until we all reach unity in the faith and in the knowledge of the Son of God and become mature, attaining to the whole measure of the fullness of Christ" (Eph. 4:11–13). (Note here that the gift of evangelist evidently was also given to build up the body.)

Thinking of ourselves as individual Christians rather than as part of a new community, leads us to read the Bible with different eyes. In an adult Sunday school class recently the teacher asked us to consider our responsibility as citizens. He gave us a worksheet that noted verses about our being "aliens and strangers," called on to "pray for those in authority," to be completely faithful in civil obligations, to expose evil, to do what is good, to bless those who do evil to us, and to withdraw from the world when necessary. After some opening remarks, each group was asked to discuss the implications for us as Christians.

When the groups were asked to report on their discussions, without exception the responses were in terms of the individual. Each group read the verses as though they were addressed to individuals only, never considering that the Epistles of the New Testament were written to *churches.* How different the responses might have been if we had responded as a group. What power we could have as a community. How weak we so often feel as individuals.

The conviction of many evangelicals that God not only has a sovereign will and a moral will for humanity, but that He also has an *individual* will for each of us is the other side of this coin. Thus we hear Christians talking about "God's plan for your life," causing us to picture a one-of-a-kind blueprint. Many believe God has worked out ahead of time all the details of the life we are to lead as individuals and that our task is to discover God's individual will for our lives. When we fail, we must admit having to accept "God's second best." I will not take time here to argue this point, since Garry Friesen has done so well in *Decision Making & the Will of God,* except to comment that this is almost a peculiarly American doctrine.

Reading God's Word as though we are searching for His will for us as individuals instead of His will for us as a community, can have a strange effect on our obedience. First, as mentioned above, we often discover a sense of powerlessness. Second, we fail to talk to one another, to stir one another up, to be obedient. Third, we decide we somehow have to "go it on our own." Thus we find Christians buying into plans for individual survival in a hostile world, such as Howard Ruff advises us in his secular book *How to Prosper During the Coming Bad Years:*

1. Store enough food for one year.
2. Have one bag of silver coins.
3. Avoid unsound debts.
4. Get rid of all big-city property.
5. Prepare for price controls in a black market economy.

And that is just what many Christians are doing. News magazines of the 1980s were filled with stories of Christian groups taking similar steps to "protect themselves." What we are not told is *how to help one another* "in the coming bad years." The evangelical church seldom mentions how we as a local community, a called-out body of believers, should face the future as a community. (I wonder what Christian brothers and sisters plan to do when fellow Christians ask for some of their hoarded resources.)

EVERYONE NEEDS TO BE MOTIVATED

Americans believe in *motivation,* a reason for doing something, and we believe this motivation should arise from within ourselves. Since Americans insist on finding the cause for an action, they also insist on finding a reason, a motivation, for *why* someone did something. We assume that any good leader must know how to motivate people, so countless books have been written on how to motivate oneself and others. Hundreds of professionals make their living by conducting motivational seminars for salesmen, who need to motivate others to buy; preachers, who need to motivate others to holy living; and just plain folks, who need to be motivated to do all the things that will make them "more effective" people.

The close relationship between our individualism and our need for internal motivation becomes even more apparent when contrasted with motivation in other cultures.

Americans find it almost impossible to believe that other peoples are motivated simply by the order of their society, the relationships between people, and the rules their society has developed for how things ought to be. We are surprised to discover that people in other societies consider it selfish to seek motivation within themselves. In fact, from the view of such a society, motivation is unnecessary; the situation speaks for itself. People who are faithful to their society need nothing more than a knowledge of the situation to do that which they ought to do. On the other hand, the more individualistic one is, the greater the need for *internal* reasons for doing something. According to David M. Potter, "Competition is the primary method among Americans of motivating members of a group and some have seen it as a basic emphasis in American culture."[3] Most other societies don't like competition. If they play a game, it is not to win, but to *play*—for fun. However, the American desire to win also means some are going to lose. The American world quickly becomes divided between "winners" and "losers."

When a senior executive of World Vision moved from New Zealand to a Latin American country, he and his wife placed their children in a school run by Americans. Thinking primarily of class structure and content in the British and American systems, I asked him how his children liked their new school. His answer surprised me. "The most difficult thing they have had to get used to is *competition.* In New Zealand everyone in the class worked to help the others because the class was judged as a whole. But in this American school everyone is competing with everyone else for good grades. It's very difficult for them to accept."

This desire to win is closely associated with a desire to acquire power for oneself. In order to "get ahead" Americans are taught to dress for success and to take courses on assertiveness training.

AN EVANGELICAL RESPONSE

On the face of it, American evangelicals believe that motivation must lie within the individual rather than the group. Our approaches to evangelism and the sales techniques we use to "stir one another up to good works" attest to our belief that if we can discover the basic needs of the *individual* and appeal to those, we can motivate him or her. Apparently we do not believe people can be motivated simply by the standards of the Word of God and of the Christian community of which they are a part.

This is a two-sided dilemma. The Bible states very

clearly that we are to understand the gifts we have been given and to use them enthusiastically. Furthermore we observe that people do best in the things they *like* to do. Putting these two thoughts together, people should be most comfortable and most enthusiastic when doing things they do well, things they like to do. In other words, people are "motivated" by things they do well. With this understanding, we can use the American concept of motivation appropriately—to help individuals find the place in the body of Christ where they can function most effectively—for the edification of the whole body, not for them as individuals.

DOING, RATHER THAN BEING

In many cultures of the world the focus is on *being* and *becoming;* the American focus, however, is on *doing.* ("How are you doing?" "I'm doing fine." "How are you coming along?") Americans believe in keeping busy. We have a need to be active, and we prefer people we describe as "active" and "energetic." It may be all right to have one or two dreamers in a society, but obviously, we cannot survive with only dreamers. After all, dreamers don't produce anything. For that is what activity is all about: to bring about change, to produce something, to make something that did not exist before. And "getting things done" leads to our excitement with technology and our need for visible results.

Thus an American may look at an Indian holy man, clad in rags and sitting cross-legged in deep thought, and never consider the *inner* dynamics of the person. The fact that the Indian may be very much at peace with himself and oblivious to the rags he is wearing makes no impression on us.

AN EVANGELICAL RESPONSE

The activism of American evangelicals causes our brothers and sisters in other countries to despair. We want instant results from our evangelistic efforts, either in numbers of decisions or in new members in the church. We have little regard for the idea that people may be strengthened *inwardly* in their relationship with the Lord and with one another; we want to see some *outward* signs.

In our attempts to communicate the gospel, we need to understand and adapt to the culture in which we are working. The reason the gospel spreads along cultural and social lines is that Christians within those cultures intuitively know how to communicate the good news with others like them. However, if we emphasize individual motivation, we may end up with individualistic churches. Somehow, our evangelism needs to direct people to a Spirit-filled motivation and away from a self-centered motivation.

American evangelicals are impatient with the absence of such activism in others. Our famous evangelists travel to such places as Nairobi, Singapore, and Madras and conduct "evangelistic campaigns," which are viewed as successful only if a large number of people respond to the invitation. The fact that our American thought forms, our American planning, and our high-powered communication techniques have little in common with the cultures we are attempting to reach never concerns us.

Many of these American evangelists would be taken aback to discover the reason for the "results" they have experienced. As one Indian Christian told me, "We want to please these evangelists, so we invite them for our yearly revival. We may have one hundred thousand people at the revival, most of whom are Christians, but when the invitation is given, a few thousand may respond. To us this is just part of our recommitment to the Lord, but we know it also pleases the evangelist, and he can go home believing he has done a good job for the Lord."

This emphasis on doing and on activity robs us of a richly rewarding inner life. Although we extol the saints of the past who believed meditation and personal Bible study were an essential part of their Christian life, we find little time for individual meditation. We glibly quote, "Man looks at the outward appearance, but the Lord looks at the heart." But then we proceed to do our very best to make sure our outward appearance is acceptable and do very little to improve our inward "appearance." In our hearts we know this is wrong, but the average American evangelical church does little to encourage us to spend time improving our inner nature. Instead of advising us to "stay home and meditate," and to "be alone before the Lord," church leaders encourage us to "come to this meeting," and to "get involved with this committee." The result often is Christians who may still look good on the outside but who are burned out on the inside. Robert Munger, a former professor of evangelism at Fuller Theological Seminary, used to take a team of students on weekends to visit and encourage local churches. At the end of the weekend they would meet with the official board of the church to ask questions. When they asked board members the question, "Since you have been serving on the church board, do you feel your spiritual life has been strengthened or weakened?" Munger was distressed to discover that almost eighty-five percent responded that their spiritual life had been weakened as a result of their "service."[4]

YOU CAN DO IT!

Visible achievement is the primary motivation for the typical middle-class American, and Americans believe that anyone who has the will can "make it." Further, we have concluded that worldly wealth is a sign of God's blessing. Whereas many other peoples of the world believe that the accumulation of possessions and wealth can only be had at the expense of others, Americans believe there is enough wealth for everyone.

> Furthermore, the achievements of the individual are not gained at the expense of others since there [are] enough rewards—material wealth, prestige, popularity—for everyone who aspires and tries. . . . Traditionally, Americans have seen failure as a lack of will and of effort on the part of the individual. Successful accumulation of worldly wealth

was a sign that the individual belonged to the select group who enjoyed the grace of God. The same idea is still present in a newer version: a rich man cannot be completely bad—or else he would not be rich.[5]

Americans not only believe this about themselves, they believe it about all the peoples of the world. They assume since "we did it, they can do it too." This produces some negative side effects in American relationships with peoples of other countries. For example, Americans may be very generous in their desire to help people who are starving, but at the same time, consciously or subconsciously, they may blame these people for having gotten themselves into the situation in the first place. Therefore, a great deal of our generosity is done with an attitude of a superior giving to an inferior. We fail to see that the accident of history that created a famine is no different from the accident of history that created America. As we will see, this dominant American belief in unlimited available wealth, which has endured for two hundred and fifty years, may now be faced with a new reality.

AN EVANGELICAL RESPONSE

The basic appeals of American evangelicalism are to the individual. We emphasize individual salvation and the individual's ability to accept and appropriate God's gift of salvation by grace.

Our acceptance of individualism allows us to feel quite comfortable with the American tradition of "rugged individualism." The American message, and too often the evangelical message, is filled with phrases like the following: "*You* are the captain of your fate, the master of your soul." "Anyone can 'make it' in America." "Anyone can be wealthy, or at least comfortably middle-class." "God blessed America, and He wants to bless you." Notice how easily we as evangelicals equate worldly wealth with God's blessing.

Consequently, in our evangelistic efforts we too often

present Jesus as the missing dimension in life, a dimension which, if filled, will make a person "the compleat American," i.e., "Come to Jesus and have it *all.*"

We "rich" Americans have easily concluded that what we have has come from our own efforts. After all, each day we are called on to "make it on our own." We have been encouraged to become an active participant in our own culture because our culture assumes we *can* do something. We believe, as Stewart said, "a rich man cannot be completely bad—or else he would not be rich."

There is no need to elaborate on this theme. The problem of deference to the rich is not peculiarly American. Jesus had some hard things to say about the difficulties rich people would have in entering the kingdom. The failure of American evangelicalism is its quiet acceptance of this unspoken doctrine that equates success with the blessing of God.

Ron Sider has written a provocative book, *Rich Christians in an Age of Hunger,* exploring this idea. It has been interesting to observe the response to it. Some "evangelical" Christians are so appalled by his ideas about riches and poverty that they felt it necessary to write a response to it in a book with a cover identical, except for the title, to Sider's book.

NOTES

[1]Edward C. Stewart, *American Cultural Patterns: A Cross-Cultural Perspective* (LaGrange Park: Intercultural Press, 1971),   32.

[2]Robert Webber, *Common Roots: A Call to Evangelical Maturity* (Grand Rapids: Zondervan, 1978),   49.

[3]Stewart, *American Cultural Patterns,*   42.

[4]For an effective aid to strengthen your personal spiritual life, see Richard J. Foster, *Celebration of Discipline: Paths to Spiritual Growth* (New York: Harper and Row, 1978).

[5]Stewart, *American Cultural Patterns,*   44.

CHAPTER 5

American Relationships

> *When the inhabitant of a democratic country compares himself individually with all those about him, he feels with pride that he is the equal of any of them.*   De Tocqueville

Americans are friendly people but, according to Edward C. Stewart, they "rarely form deep and lasting friendships." He further states that "although social activities occupy much of his [the American's] time, he avoids personal commitments to others. He does not like to get involved."

GETTING INVOLVED WITH PEOPLE

Other societies have a deep need for enduring and comprehensive friendships, but Americans seldom develop this type of relationship. We make friendships as a function of roles. We have office friends, business friends, tennis friends, shopping friends, and church friends. Australians will put friends before their company; Americans will assume the company or the cause comes before friendship.

AN EVANGELICAL RESPONSE

Like most Americans, American evangelicals make friends easily. But our friendships are often based on the roles we play, and we are just as guilty of failing to make deep and lasting friendships as are our unbelieving neighbors. Even in our small groups we hesitate to make long-lasting commitments. And when we do make commitments, too often they are based on the performances of others, rather than on an unconditional commitment to the individual as a person.

American evangelicals live in a mobile society. Twenty-five percent of Americans change their address every year. Moving from one locality to another necessitates moving from one local church to another. For most evangelical Christians who move, shopping for a new church is their first order of business. But the decision of which church to join is more likely to be based on what the individual and the family can receive *from* the church than on what the family can give *to* the church as each family member exercises his or her spiritual gifts.

Very seldom does our commitment to a local church affect our decision of whether or not to move to a new location. Instead, better financial opportunity is the most common consideration. We do not see our commitment to the local church and to one another as the *center of our universe*, but as adjunct. When we get down to the bottom line, we are more committed to the secular company for which we work than we are to the local church to which we claim to be related.

In fact, our church situation may be part of our reason for moving. Indeed, "burned out" Christians, those who have become so active in their local church that they have had no time for themselves or for their families, often seek a church in a new town where they can remain anonymous and simply enjoy the services for a while.

EVERYONE IS EQUAL

In one sense, Americans believe everyone is equal. We dislike people who use authority or rank for personal advantage. But this basic American tenet conflicts with our view of motivation and success as well as with our desire to be treated as individuals with special characteristics. John Gardner dealt with the first part of this tension in his book *Excellence.* The subtitle of Gardner's book captures it well: *Can We Be Equal and Excellent Too?* Americans are particularly adept at dealing with such contradictions. We try to work our way out of this equal versus excellent dilemma with phrases like "Everyone is equal, but some are more equal than others." We are pragmatists. We want a value system that works. The fact that it has contradictions within itself is of small importance.

The tension between equality and superiority is exemplified in our uneasiness with bureaucracies. Bureaucracies, by definition, are established to deal with everyone as equals. In theory, everyone is treated the same. But when confronted by such a bureaucracy, we feel as though we are "being treated like a number."[1] We want everyone else to be treated equally, but *we* want to be treated specially, or "more equally."

AN EVANGELICAL RESPONSE

The American idea that everyone is equal flows naturally into our church life. Most of us agree that it is a positive American value. In fact, that it is a very Christian one. The Bible tells us not to think of ourselves more highly than we ought (Rom. 12:3) and not to exalt ourselves over one another but to care for one another. But the Bible goes further by saying, "those parts of the body that seem to be weaker are indispensable, and the parts that we think are less honorable we treat with special honor.... God has combined the members of the body and has given greater honor to the parts that lacked it...." (1 Cor. 12:22–24). How upside down from the way the world views things! Imagine a fellowship in which the members would constantly seek to bestow honor on those members of the congregation who "seem less honorable," those who are seldom in the limelight but who fulfill an important, though unglamorous, role in the body. Think what would happen. Instead of the same people receiving honor time after time, the whole body would be honored.

CONFRONTATION

Many other societies believe so strongly in not hurting another's feelings that individuals go to great lengths to "save face." But Americans believe in confrontation, in "getting it out on the table." Some years ago, in my typically American way, I had a confrontation with an Indian brother. I felt that the path he wanted to pursue would result in difficulty for all of us, but particularly for him. So, during a meeting with eight or nine people, in my eagerness to be helpful, I said, "Brother, if you keep going in this direction you are headed for trouble. It just won't work. You're wrong!"

A number of months later my friend was finally able to share with me how deeply he had been wounded by my outspokenness and apparent insensitivity to him, especially in front of others. He explained to me that because of his cultural background it would be a number of years before he would be able to erase the memory of how I had hurt him. He was right. It took us over two years to rebuild our friendship.

AN EVANGELICAL RESPONSE

American evangelicals also believe in "telling it like it is." We believe it is better to express our feelings about another's failure, to be done with it, and to put it in the past. In many ways this seems to follow Christ's instructions to His disciples as to what to do if a brother sins against you:

> If your brother sins against you, go and show him his fault, just between the two of you. If he listens to you, you have won your brother over. But if he will not listen, take one or two others along, so that "every matter may be established by the testimony of two or three witnesses." If he refuses to listen to them, tell it to the church; and if he

refuses to listen even to the church, treat him as you would a pagan or a tax collector (Matt. 18:15–17).

Confrontation of this type is biblical, as long as we remember all the other biblical injunctions to right living. Biblical confrontation starts with "just between the two of you" but is controlled by all other dimensions of Christian ethics. Biblical confrontation does not put people in their place. It reaches out in love. Tough love, if you will. But love.

Confrontation plays a major role in much of our personal evangelism. *Evangelism Explosion* by James Kennedy teaches us to call on people "cold turkey" and talk to them about their salvation. "If you died tonight, would you go to heaven?" we are instructed to ask virtual strangers. Never mind if they are hurting over a wayward son or a lost job. They need to meet Jesus right now. (And of course my critics will give me another typically American response: "But it works!")

FAIR PLAY

The American belief in what we call fair play has probably come from our view of life as a contest or a game. We teach our children at a young age that they are to play by the rules. We assume that the rules are right and that they should be observed. The rules may change in the future; but whatever they are at a particular time, they are to be obeyed.

Similarly, we live by a set of laws that allows us to pursue our own goals while cooperating with others who have their own goals. This is a peculiar American value, and the fact that other cultures do not have this same value often troubles us. Middle-class Americans generally will not respond to what we would call such abstract ideas as "dignity of man" or "honor." But an appeal to our spirit of fair play will easily invoke a response because fair play includes our attempts to accommodate the weaknesses of others, an important aspect of our "everyone is equal" culture.

This belief in fair play also helps explain why it is so difficult for Americans to understand those in other cultures who "exploit" their power or position. Americans go to great lengths to let everyone have his or her say and to avoid unfairness. Our whole concept of democracy is based on this understanding. Therefore, when we see leaders in other societies making decisions without consulting their followers, we label them dictators, which to us is an unacceptable form of leadership.

AN EVANGELICAL RESPONSE

The overall idea of fair play appears to be quite biblical. As Christians we are taught to accommodate those who are weak and are admonished not to do anything that will hurt a weaker brother or sister (1 Cor. 8:11–13).

But the concept on which fair play is based, that life is a game, is not biblical. Unfortunately, however, the "life is a game" philosophy has infiltrated much of evangelical thinking. "Winning souls" is considered the ultimate mark of the good Christian. We hold "crusades." We run Sunday school contests. (I was responsible for a city-wide attendance contest in Grand Rapids many years ago!) We award prizes for doing well. But accepting this type of win-lose competition has some serious complications. It's hard to talk about being a servant to everyone when we are out to beat them.

The further implication of fair play, that everyone should be allowed to hold his or her own opinion, also presents some serious problems. On the surface it seems plausible, but it will eventually cause tension because Christians don't believe everyone can be right. American pluralism is possible only because Americans are willing to be democratic, to allow others to have their own beliefs, and to submit to majority opinion. Such is not the case with Christians. Though we tolerate differing opinions, our tolerance becomes a basis for division rather than for unity. As a result, this tolerance can keep us from attempting a reconciliation with Christians with whom we disagree.

So even though fair play and tolerance are important and essential aspects of our American democratic society, when carried over to the evangelical community, these concepts can disrupt fellowship and make long-lasting commitments virtually impossible.

AMERICANS WANT TO BE LIKED

Americans have a tremendous need to be liked. Indeed, our self-esteem is based on how much others like us. Because of this strong desire, we have difficulty understanding why others do not appreciate our overtures of friendship and concern. *The Ugly American*, published in 1958, gave us one of our first clues as to why our generosity to our enemies at the end of a world war was not accepted with overwhelming love and gratitude.[2]

Americans tend to judge their personal and social success by their popularity. The author of one popular book on dealing with stress holds forth the notion that the best way to live in a society full of stress is to accumulate the appreciation of others.[3] In a society of people who judge themselves by how many friends they have and by how many people like them, the people who are most liked and have the largest number of friends will experience the least amount of stress.

AN EVANGELICAL RESPONSE

Americans want to be liked, and evangelicals are no exception. We put great importance on being accepted by others. American evangelicals rejoice when a prominent Christian, such as Billy Graham, is entertained at the White House. When some well-known individual becomes "one of us," we publicize the news. Our churches attempt to be "friendly places where all are welcome."

Perhaps that is why we find so few prophets among modern American evangelicals. The Old Testament prophets were those who were God's mouthpieces. They stood on the side of justice, on the side of the poor. They stood against the corruption of their society. Where are the evangelicals of former years who were willing to expose an unpopular cause even though others might dislike them?

I remember a time I was teaching an adult Sunday school class when our city was deep in an interracial conflict. A school-board election was coming up. As one who had some understanding of the way American blacks had been treated through the years, I spoke passionately about the need to be involved as Christians with one side of the issue. I received more negative phone calls as a result of that "outburst" than from any other lesson I ever taught! Being prophetic is not popular!

INTROSPECTION AND SELF-CRITICISM

Probably no society in the world is as self-critical and self-judging as America. The very openness that others find so hard to accept in the American manner is applied equally to everything in our society. The American penchant for "investigative reporting," once called muckraking, is evident everywhere. As astounding as Watergate was to America, equally astounding to many other nations was that Americans got all excited about it.

Americans are continually probing and pushing into every corner of everyday life, criticizing, judging, expecting to find something that can be made better. Self-criticism is expected and highly valued.

AN EVANGELICAL RESPONSE

When it comes to introspection and self-criticism as an American value, we have good news and bad news for American evangelicals. The good news is that we are willing to look at ourselves objectively, expecting to find something that needs improving. Knowing that we are complete in Christ and yet realizing that the sinful nature is still very much a part of us is a healthy balance.

The bad news is that our introspection often keeps us

from resting in the Lord. We have the assurance God loves us, but we have a sneaking suspicion He doesn't *like* us.

An interesting aside to the evangelical's working out of this American value is our willingness to criticize ourselves as *individuals*, but our hesitancy to criticize our evangelical institutions. It is hard for us to make value judgments of Christian organizations which, in our eyes, "have been raised of God." Consequently, we often find ourselves easily misled by propaganda parading as an announcement of God's will. Perhaps the recent formation of the Evangelical Council for Financial Accountability, an organization dedicated to full disclosure of the financial practices of Christian organizations, is a move in a corrective direction.

ROLES

American society separates social and occupational roles differently from any other culture. Literally, Americans work so they can play. Many other societies don't see any difference. They enjoy what Americans call "play" just as much as they enjoy what Americans call "work." This is not to suggest that they believe all of life is enjoyable, nor that it is all play, but to point out that Americans have been taught that play is enjoyable and work is not.

This American desire to differentiate between work and play is closely related to the American concept of commitment. We tend to make limited commitments and to make those commitments based on the individual roles we play. If I see myself as playing a number of different roles, rather than as an integrated whole, I cannot commit all of myself to anything. Commitment can go no further than role.

AN EVANGELICAL RESPONSE

Americans see themselves as playing many different roles, and so do American evangelicals. We have often read stories about the deacon who acted righteous on Sunday but who was a dishonest businessman the rest of the week. Seeing ourselves as playing different roles allows us to avoid becoming Christians at the core of life. Rather than seeing our Christian life as fundamental to every other part of life, too often we see it as just another role we play. Instead of being slaves of Christ we demand the *rights* of our citizenship in the kingdom. Instead of seeing all of life as part of kingdom life, our citizenship is a part-time affair. We are very much like citizens of one country who hold passports to another: they have potential citizenship in two countries. Many of us need to burn one of our passports and make a lifetime commitment to a group of fellow citizens.

Americans live in a society based on limited or partial commitments. We move very easily between commitments to work, family, club, and to an organization we call the church. In analyzing this situation, Robert Webber says,

> A major problem among many evangelicals is the failure to have an incarnational understanding of the church. This failure has caused many to view the church as a social institution, a psychiatrist's couch, an evangelistic tent, or a lecture hall. The current attempt to bring renewal by putting chairs in a circle, singing with a guitar, meeting in homes, and studying the Bible in small groups without the rediscovery of the incarnational nature of the church may be less the beginning of renewal than the last gasp before death.[4]

Christians see themselves as members of an organization rather than as part of a physical body. As noted above, the familiar metaphor of the church being the body of Christ and of individuals in it being related to one another in the same way different parts of a body are related is, for most evangelicals, an abstraction rather than a reality.

To truly believe that we are members of Christ's body, and that in some mysterious way we are something other people are not, is a very difficult idea for the average American to understand. American pluralism, the multi-plication of churches, our inability to hold a belief in one, true, *visible* church all work against our accepting ourselves as incarnate members of Christ's body.

NOTES

[1]For a thorough description of this phenomenon, see Peter Berger, et al., *Homeless Mind: Modernization and Consciousness* (New York: Irvington, 1973). In Berger's mind, the notions of bureaucracy and technology are the dominant shapers of American thinking.

[2]See William J. Lederer and Eugene Burdick, *The Ugly American* (New York: Norton, 1958). This book caused a wave of self-analysis when it appeared.

[3]See Hans Selye, *Stress Without Distress* (New York: Harper and Row, 1974).

[4]Robert Webber, *Common Roots: A Call to Evangelical Maturity* (Grand Rapids: Zondervan, 1978), 51.

CHAPTER 6

What's the World Like, America?

I accost an American sailor, and inquire why the ships of his country are built so as to last but for a short time; he answers without hesitation, that the art of navigation is every day making such rapid progress, that the finest vessel would become almost useless if it lasted beyond a few years.

De Tocqueville

In American thinking, being human has certain values that are different from the values of other forms of life. Americans see themselves as separated from nature and all other forms of life. The rest of the world is seen as having life, but it is mechanistic and material. Someone has observed that although the British may walk about the world as though they own it, Americans walk about the world as if they do not care *who* owns it! Whereas many cultures see humans as just another form of life, differing only in degree, Americans see humans as standing above the rest of life.

Not only are humans outstanding, they are basically perfectible because of their humanness.

While religion in the United States is committed to the doctrine that man is evil by nature, most Americans are unlikely to give the concept much thought. More likely they will see man as a mixture of good and evil or [as] a creature of his environment and experience. Most important, they will stress his ability to change. . . . The belief in the perfectibility of man and in progress seems more characteristic of Americans than does the belief that man is innately evil. Doctrines of human nature are overshadowed by the view of man's ability to change his environment and to be affected by it. Man can change, improve himself, and it is his responsibility to do so.[1]

An Eastern view of the world might stress the unity of all forms of life, with man an integral part of nature in harmony with the physical world. Americans believe the physical world should be controlled in the service of humankind. Americans take an engineering approach to a world based on technology. Attempts to apply this technology, even in the realm of social dynamics (human engineering), are the result of believing that natural laws governing the physical world can be harnessed to produce material welfare, an enhancer at the service of humankind.[2] This idea may well have its origin in the interpretation of the creation narrative that sees humankind as having been given the role of *dominating* the earth rather than the role of steward of its resources.

PROGRESS

Associated with the technological control of the environment is the American idea of progress. Things can be "better." They will be better. Better can mean many different things. "Most Americans tend to believe the basic problems of the world are technological and their solution will bring about economic welfare. Economics is the final arbiter of the good and desirable. Progress, then, quite often means the achievement of physical comfort, good health (or the facilities for giving medical care), material possessions and a high standard of living."[3]

Until quite recently Americans have been basically optimistic about the future and about our individual ability to successfully make our way into the future. An underlying and key assumption here is that there is enough material wealth in the world for everyone. Although other societies may believe in the idea of "Limited Good,"[4] which means that if I get more you have to get less, Americans are free from this notion. They are therefore able to progress both individually and corporately without feeling that their success may be at the expense of another.

Imbedded in this idea of progress is resistance to any thought that there may *not* be a solution for today's or tomorrow's problem. Notice the logical, ultimate result of such reasoning: If all problems are ultimately solvable, then humans are ultimately in control of their own destiny. The God of creation may still be needed as an explanation of the initial cause, but the God of miracles is no longer needed.

The idea of progress is not new, but only in America has it reached a standard of a given truth. It has been the engine behind many of our country's recognizable accomplishments. We will not take the time here to trace this belief back to its roots in the thinking of early American Christians, but we should not overlook the positive dimensions of an innate optimism about the future.

In his milestone book *History of the Idea of Progress*, Richard Nisbet points to a weakening of this view of progress as a major threat to American life. Interestingly, his one note of hope is the possibility of a spiritual revival. A revival, he says, will restore the loss of hope engendered by a vision of the past that sees nothing but failure in our despoiling of the earth, our murderous "police actions," and our dwindling resources.

AN EVANGELICAL RESPONSE

The concept of progress fits naturally into the Christian view of history, which pictures humankind as moving toward a culmination, the blessed hope. The promise of Christ's second coming and of the establishment of a new heaven and a new earth gives the Christian a straightline view of history that is essentially optimistic.

At the same time we see the individual as a growing person, "maturing in Christ." We are admonished to become mature men and women and are told that as a local expression of Christ's church we should also mature. But this is not a maturity in material things. It is a maturity of the Spirit, a maturity of relationships between one another and between ourselves and our Lord.

The question that lies before us as American evangelicals is whether our optimism about the future is based on our own confidence in American technology or on our confidence in the God of creation. As Nisbet has pointed out, what we decide as evangelicals may well determine the future of our country.

WHAT ABOUT PEOPLE?

As we noted earlier, it is very difficult for Americans to believe that people in other cultures make no distinction between the individual self and the group self. To an American "the self" is *me*. The world therefore is perceived from a very individualistic viewpoint. The individual becomes the basic reference for living. Children are encouraged to "make their own way" and to "stand on their own feet." We assume that everyone has complete freedom of choice and autonomy. Independence is the goal of both young and old.

But though Americans perceive themselves as individuals, American *individualism* is something quite different. Individualism is fundamental to the quality of self-reliance. In reality this is a myth, for we are obviously completely dependent on one another. But the need for self-reliance remains, and it is peculiarly American.[5]

> The meaning of the value [of self-reliance] is neither translatable nor self-evident in other cultures. For example, in the Spanish of Latin America, self-reliance is translated as "independence" and carries the suggestion of political

and social freedom as well as the implication of solitary action, but the idea of the self as the source and sole limiting factor is missing. These ideas are not congenial to the Latin who has a strong attachment to his family and immediate group. Dependence is not deplored by him as it is by Americans. And among the Chinese, dependence on others is desirable for it strengthens the relationship among people. Chinese parents, for instance, take pride in being dependent on their children and supported by them in a manner to which they are *unaccustomed* [italics mine].[6]

AN EVANGELICAL RESPONSE

American evangelicals have to struggle to see themselves as an integral part of a larger entity, a group. One of the reasons American churches find the biblical concept of the body of Christ so difficult to understand and to appropriate is the American focus on self as completely coincident with the individual. We read what the Bible says about being part of a body, but in our mind this body is made up of unique parts (individuals) fitted together. But a body is not like that. You may be a hand, and I may be an elbow, but who has ever seen a hand or an elbow living by itself? Can an elbow or a hand refer to itself as "me?" Are they not both nurtured by the circulation system and the nervous system of the "self" of which they are only a part?

When missionaries report "people movements," in which large numbers of people within a culture become Christians at the same time, we have an uneasy feeling that these people may have missed a *personal* commitment to the Savior. Personal conversion, we believe, is more likely to result in personal (individual) growth because we don't see ourselves as growing together as part of a larger body, but as individuals responsible for our own growth and maturing in Christ. Even those who desire to "disciple" others focus on the growth of the individual, often to the exclusion of how and where the person's spiritual gifts and experience should fit into the body of Christ.

The Bible comes at it differently. "Instead, speaking the truth in love, we will in all things grow up into Him who is the Head, that is, Christ. From Him the whole body, joined and held together by every supporting ligament, grows and builds itself up in love, as each part does its work" (Eph. 4:15–16).

The evangelical focus on individual and personal salvation has another dimension: it keeps us from understanding what Christians in other parts of Christ's church are saying about corporate salvation. Saving *a soul* (an individual) becomes the ultimate goal of evangelical evangelism. We naively assume that once individuals are in the kingdom they will act not only for the good of the body of Christ, but for the good of all humankind. But the Bible speaks just as strongly about the salvation of the community. Israel was a chosen *people.* The new Israel, the church, is a community. Protestants call individuals *out of the world,* but Roman Catholics call them *into the community* where God has prepared a place for them.

> But you are a chosen people, a royal priesthood, a holy nation, a people belonging to God, that you may declare the praises of him who called you out of darkness into his wonderful light. Once you were not a people, but now you are the people of God; once you had not received mercy, but now you have received mercy (1 Pet. 2:9–10).

The work of this community is to be salt and light *in the world* and to speak words of prophetic judgment on injustice and all forms of wickedness.

CHANGE

American culture has institutionalized change as has no other society. This willingness to change, to discard the past, colors the American view of the world. This is why of all societies American society can be termed the most "modernizing." People in a traditional society assume that tomorrow will be like today. We have always done things the same way, so tomorrow will be no different from today. In a modernizing society people are open to accepting changes and restrictions that would have been unthinkable in years past. For example, Americans seem to be more willing to place themselves in the hands of government or of an organization than Americans of a generation ago. Along this same line, we have willingly given up some of our individualism in the redefining of sex roles. In recent years middle-class America has been willing to put aside its traditional insistence on sexual difference between male and female.[7]

Coupled with this acceptance of change is the notion that modern thought is superior to all past forms of understanding reality. We describe ourselves as being in a "knowledge revolution" and often quote those who say statistics prove that the amount of knowledge accumulated in the past generation exceeds all knowledge accumulated in generations of prior history. (What we fail to see, of course, is the difference between knowledge and wisdom.) And the unfortunate result is that parents *expect* not to be able to understand what their children are learning in school and easily believe that they have nothing to teach their children.

Consequently, we have a society that places extreme importance on youth and little value on age. Whereas individuals in other societies may look forward to growing old and to gaining esteem, Americans dread old age and try to put it off at all costs.

The real value of the accumulated wisdom of a lifetime is that it can be handed on to future generations. Our society, however, has lost its conception of wisdom and knowledge, according to which technological change constantly renders knowledge obsolete and therefore non-transferable. The older generation has nothing to teach the younger, nor emotional and intellectual resources to make its own choices and to deal with "unstructured" situations for which there are not reliable precedent or precepts. It is taken for granted that children will quickly learn to find their parents old-fashioned and out-of-date, and parents themselves tend to accept the social definition of their own superfluity.[8]

In a real sense society has accepted the idea that what is new in culture is better than what is old. According to Daniel Bell, this tendency is reflected in various art forms:

> What is singular about this "tradition of the new" is that it allows art to be unfettered, to break down all genres and to explore all modes of experience sensation. Fantasy today has few costs (Is anything deemed bizarre or unspeakable today?) other than the rush of individual madness.[9]

The role of the artist has first been legitimatized and thus exalted so that we are free to explore all that may be new and different. The "new" is the expected norm.

AN EVANGELICAL RESPONSE

The Christian view of change, like our view of progress, places us in a dialectical dilemma from which most of us would like to escape. We should be open to change, if change means spiritual growth. At the same time, if change means forgetting the past, our spiritual foundation and roots, then we will lose the anchor that can hold us firm. The question of changing to meet the needs of the church and the world we are called to minister to falls somewhere between these two extremes.

David Hubbard tells the story of a little boy who lived near him. He was so recalcitrant that his mother had him tethered to a tree so he would not wander off. Perhaps anticipating the day of behavior modification, she had a winch on the tree to reel him in. When she did this, she would call, "Johnny, Johnny." Johnny would come backing and yelling up to the tree. How like so many Christians, Hubbard observes. They come backing and screaming into the future, trying to hold on to the past. Of all people Christians should be open to the future, open to change. Our past is forgiven. Our future is secure. But often, in our desire to conserve the fundamentals, we demand stability for its own sake. Have you ever heard a discussion about a proposed organizational change in a local church that started (or ended!) with, "Well, it was good enough for the founders of this church so it ought to be good enough for us!"?

But change that forgets our history can be devastating. We do have what Robert Webber calls "common roots," and we need to remember the past. God did not stop teaching us when the Bible was completed. We have a Christian heritage that should shape and mold our future. The biblical model is to look backward and recount the acts of God, so we can look forward with confidence. For this reason, the writer of Acts thought it very important to tell us everything Stephen said to his accusers. How easy it would have been for Luke simply to have said, "He [Stephen] reminded them of their history, all the times they had turned from God," and then said, "You stiff-necked people. . . ." But Luke recorded much more than that. In Acts 7:1–50, Luke recounts in detail the whole history of Israel as Stephen spoke it before the Sanhedrin. This emphasizes the tremendous importance of witnessing to one another of what God has done.

The world acts as though yesterday is just the rubbish heap upon which today is to be built. For Christians, however, the life and teachings of yesterday's saints and apostles are part of the foundation of our faith. Robert Webber made the following analysis: "The major issue facing evangelical Christianity, the one from which all other problems flow, is a kind of evangelical amnesia. Evangelicals have forgotten the past. There is a need to change what Bernard Ramm calls our 'sadly deficient' state of historical knowledge."[10]

One young woman summarized our dilemma well when she recently said to my pastor, "I seem to be losing my hindsight." How we desperately need hindsight. We need to remember what God has taught us, not only through his

Word but through the host of witnesses who have gone before.

Another unfortunate dimension of evangelicals and change is our willingness to change our actions without changing our beliefs. To put it another way, we keep holding on to beliefs upon which we no longer act. Our beliefs themselves become sacrosanct, idols placed upon a shelf to be preserved rather than truths to be lived.

THE DENIAL OF DEATH

The emphasis on youth in American society is accompanied by an attempt to deny the existence of the aged (we isolate them in "senior citizen homes" and convalescent hospitals),[11] which ultimately leads us to deny death itself. This denial takes place in two steps: the first is fear of the process of dying; the second is the fear of death itself.

In an article in *Christian Century* entitled "The Anxiety Runner: Terminal Helplessness," W. Fred Graham points out that our ancestors scarcely knew the anxiety of terminal illness. When they became sick, they quickly died. But with our modern ability to keep people alive, the thought of languishing slowly in a convalescent home is too much for us. It is the ultimate feeling of helplessness.[12]

In the same article, Graham quoted a runner he knew who said, "I'm going to run until I'm 90. If the weather is bad on my last day, I'll collapse and die on the indoor track. Don't let anyone try to keep me alive, Fred. Just take a push broom and shove me off the running surface. Then when you've finished your end, call a coroner."

The second denial of American culture, the denial of death, has been spelled out well by Ernest Becker in his book *Denial of Death*.[13] Human beings are the only creatures who *understand* that one day they are going to die. Only humans know and understand mortality. For this reason we fear death; it is the ultimate indication of our helplessness. The American response to such helplessness is to deny it by attempting to make it as harmless as possible and to keep it at arm's length. The studies done on death and dying by Kubler-Ross and others have made us aware that terminally ill patients are often placed as far away as possible from nursing stations in hospitals. They have also given us new understanding of our fear of even admitting to a dying relative that death is close at hand.[14]

AN EVANGELICAL RESPONSE

Obviously, Christians do not deny the reality of death. But it is not difficult to demonstrate how we attempt to avoid the *pain* of death. In assuring ourselves and those who grieve that a loved one is now "with the Lord," we deny our humanness and the tragedy of death's destruction of our community and our family relationships. Again we see our individualism coming to the fore. If each of us is considered an individual, then it's quite simple to deal with each individual abstractly, as a separate entity. If, on the other hand, we see that we are closely related as members of something so intimate that the Bible could only call it a body, then we have some idea what it means to experience loss through death. If a friend lost a hand, would we comfort him by telling him that someday he would be made whole in heaven? How then can we glibly assure people that their relationships will be made whole again in heaven and ignore the ultimate pain of the separation of death?

MATERIAL COMFORT

Americans have a strong desire to be materially well off and physically comfortable.

> They expect swift and convenient transportation—preferably controlled by themselves—a variety of clean and healthful foods and comfortable homes equipped with numerous labor-saving devices, certainly including central heating and hot water. The Government is expected to ensure that food and drug products meet acceptable standards and that appropriate public health measures are

observed by all people and agencies whose activites can affect the public's welfare. Associated with the values of physical comfort and health is the acceptance of cleanliness as being nearly identical with health, if not with "Godliness."[15]

How did we manage to survive without air-conditioned automobiles? What would we do if there were no service organizations to call when we need help?

The first time I was entertained in a middle-class British home, I was dismayed to discover the family heated only the living room. Evidently the thought that it was necessary to heat bedrooms had never entered their minds.

> Americans tend to project this complex of values, centering around comfort and material well-being, to other peoples. They assume that given the opportunity, everyone else would be just like themselves. Hence, they are disturbed by the sight of the rich churches of Latin America standing in the midst of poverty, the Buddhist meditating among the suffering and the rejection of American values throughout much of the world by men whose concepts of life are esthetic and spiritual.[16]

AN EVANGELICAL RESPONSE

American evangelicals have certainly bought into the American value of comfort. Being at ease in Zion to us means being free from physical discomfort, pain, stress, and the hurts of living in an everyday world. We focus on the "victorious Christian life" and hold up as our models the giants of faith whom we find in the first part of the eleventh chapter of Hebrews. Very seldom do we hear sermons preached on the second half of that same chapter:

> Others were tortured and refused to be released, so that they might gain a better resurrection. Some faced jeers and flogging, while still others were chained and put in prison. They were stoned; they were sawed in two; they were put to death by the sword. They went about in sheepskins and goatskins, destitute, persecuted and mistreated—the world

was not worthy of them. They wandered in deserts and mountains, and in caves and holes in the ground (Heb. 11:35–38).

We marvel at the ability of churches to prosper under persecution in countries where there is little religious freedom and find it difficult to believe that God may be just as much at work in times of poverty and persecution as He is in times of prosperity and plenty.

By focusing on the material comfort of individuals, we have little to say about the "comfort"of the church in being salt and light in the world. Since our desire is to feel good about ourselves, we easily respond to the world's message that *things* are more important than people. Advertisements in Christian magazines tell us that we too can have "the good life." And, as is usually the case, we find biblical justification for the material abundance preachers promise and we eagerly accumulate. After all, does not Matthew 6:33 tell us that "all these things will be given to you as well"? (How easy it is to eliminate the first part of the verse: "But seek first his kingdom and his righteousness.") It is the trick of the Devil to make us believe that desire is adequate justification for acquiring things. Most of us are all too willing to be fooled. Perhaps the ultimate evidence is the Christian charm school.

> To make sure that when Christian women turn the other cheek they will radiate the appropriate Christian beauty, there are the Patricia French Christian Charm Schools and Patricia French Cosmetics. The schools cater to Christian women of all ages who desire to improve their poise, voice, diction, personality, social graces and appearance. Patricia French Cosmetics, in turn, are made especially for Christian women.[17]

AVOIDANCE

Accompanying materialism and the emphasis on self is the tactic of *avoidance*. Avoid being hurt by avoiding commitment. Do not get involved with the world; it is a hurting world. Do not listen to the statistics. Do not be concerned about the true dimensions of the larger world in which we live. Do not face the reasons for poverty or the reality of how many people starve to death each day. The real physical world is depressing. It makes us feel guilty and embarrassed. Avoid commitment to the local church. If we do not like one, there is always another down the street that perhaps will better meet our needs. (My Episcopalian father, who faithfully served as a warden at his church for over thirty years, used to call such church-hopping "worshipping a pair of pants.") Avoid commitments in marriage. Perhaps the idea of trial marriage is not so bad after all. If it does not work out it is nice to think there could be some way other than divorce to get out of the problem.

Avoidance is closely coupled with living in the "now." If we can live for now, we can avoid thinking about the future. Postpone as many decisions as possible. In observing the American scene, Gail Sheehy has concluded in her book *Pathfinders* that this is the "postponing generation."[18] The parental question of twenty-five years ago, "What are you going to be or do with your life?" is out of vogue. The world is such a big and scary place that we hesitate to make any decisions that will have ultimate consequences.

AN EVANGELICAL RESPONSE

As in everything that has gone before, we are forced to generalize, to give overall impressions. Not all Christians are trying the avoidance tactic, any more than all evangelical Christians fit the descriptive comparisons we have made with American culture.

But like most Americans we have been so numbed by the impact of the horror of war and starvation brought into our living rooms on the evening news that we can no longer feel. As we sit as *individuals* and watch, we are overcome by a great sense of helplessness. What can we do? How can we make a difference? And we know instinctively that we cannot. As individuals we are powerless. So we avoid thinking about it.

We avoid thinking about the more than *two billion* people in the world who will never hear the Good News of salvation unless some Christians somewhere cross cultural and language barriers to reach them. Two billion people going to hell; that's too much to think about.[19] We can't handle it.

Nor can most of us handle the poverty and lower-class culture that surrounds so many of our old downtown churches. Lower-class people are scary. They don't speak our language. We might get hurt. Our kids might get hurt. Let the professionals reach them.

THE LOSS OF THE SACRED

This hardly seems the place to end a discussion on American culture. The sacred seems to lie in the domain of the church, or at least in religion. But the idea of gods who were "out there," who were forces loose in the world who could somehow hold things together, has been with humankind since the beginning. The notion that there is something sacred, a place or situation into which we dare not enter, has had a significant hold on the thinking of all the world. After all, it is the sacred that gives meaning to life, all life. To no longer believe there is anything "out there" beyond us, that all we have is what lies at our feet, is a terrifying thought indeed.

America was founded on the concept of the sacred. "Godliness" was built into our society, into our way of thinking. Somewhere along the way we lost it as an *experience*, but we continued to claim it as a part of our heritage. We continued to live life as though godliness were a reality. The present generation no longer finds it true. And, as Robert Nisbet points out, "the sacred [is] always at the heart of any genuine culture—from ancient Athens to Victorian England.[20]

AN EVANGELICAL RESPONSE

Not long ago I was asked by a respected denomination to meet with a select group of leaders that was attempting to understand "the secular mind" so they could communicate with unbelievers. They were convinced that if they could understand how the secular mind thinks, they could design evangelism programs that would proclaim the Good News in thought forms the "secular mind" could understand. During our discussion I shared much of the material you have just read. I had already come to a conclusion. Our problem is not that *they* have a secular mind, whatever one might mean by that phrase; the problem is that *we*, American Christians, have a secular mind. Many of us no longer think like Christians. Our lives have been so imbedded in our society that we think pretty much like everyone else in that society.

We concluded that our problem is not how to communicate, but what we have to offer. The world is longing to believe there are groups of men and women whose commitment to one another transcends materialism, competitiveness, and *individualism*. The cost of American values is more than we can bear. We have been robbed of a sacred gift: the ability to be committed to other human beings.

We no longer speak of God's wrath and we seldom mention His awesomeness. We experience grace without law; we expect God's love without His justice. The mystery is gone. The sacred is gone.

God help us!

NOTES

[1]Edward C. Stewart, *American Cultural Patterns: A Cross-Cultural Perspective* (LaGrange Park: Intercultural Press, 1971), 61-62. The quotation is from Robin M. Williams, Jr., "American Society in Transition: Trends in Emerging Developments and Social and Cultural Systems," *Our Changing Rural Society: Perspectives and Trends*, James H. Copp, ed. (Ames: Iowa State University Press, 1964).

[2]In the early 1960s, the governor of California commissioned the aerospace industries to do some systems studies on such things as water control, smog control, and crime control. The resulting reports demonstrated conclusively how different the problems of controlling *things* are from the problems of

controlling *people.* All the reports concluded that the systems approach, the ultimate purpose of which was to place a man on the moon, was really not very helpful in controlling society.

[3]Stewart, *American Cultural Patterns,* 66.

[4]For a more detailed discussion of "Limited Good," see George M. Foster, *Traditional Cultures and the Impact of Technological Changes* (New York: Harper and Row, 1962).

[5]See Christopher Lasch, *The Culture of Narcissism: American Life in an Age of Diminishing Expectations* (New York: Norton, 1979), and Edwin Schur, *The Awareness Trap: Self Absorption Instead of Social Change* (New York: McGraw-Hill, 1977).

[6]Stewart, *American Cultural Patterns,* 72. Many attempts have been made to explain this process. In *The Fall of Public Man: The Social Psychology of Capitalism,* Richard Sennett holds forth the notion that whereas once individuals had to play public roles, both in action and in dress, they no longer have to do so. This merging of the public and private role has led to the fuzzing of lines between the formal and the informal and between male and female roles.

[7]Stewart, *American Cultural Patterns,* 77.

[8]Lasch, *The Culture of Narcissism,* 213.

[9]Daniel Bell, *The Cultural Contradictions of Capitalism* (New York: Basic, 1976), 41.

[10]Robert Webber, *Common Roots: A Call to Evangelical Maturity* (Grand Rapids: Zondervan, 1978), 15.

[11]See David Hackett Fischer, *Growing Old in America* (New York: Oxford University Press, 1978).

[12]W. Fred Graham, *Christian Century,* "The Anxiety Runner: Terminal Helplessness." August 29–September 5, 1979, 622.

[13]See Ernest Becker, *The Denial of Death* (New York: Free Press, 1973).

[14]See Elizabeth Kubler-Ross, *Questions and Answers on Death and Dying* (New York: Macmillan, 1974).

[15]Stewart, *American Cultural Patterns,* 64.

[16]Stewart *American Cultural Patterns,* 64–65.

[17]Richard Quebedeaux, *The Worldly Evangelicals* (New York: Harper and Row, 1978). 74.

[18]See Gail Sheehy, *Pathfinders* (New York: Morrow, 1981).

[19]See Edward R. Dayton, *That Everyone May Hear, Third Edition* (Monrovia: MARC, 1983).

[20]Robert Nisbet, *History of the Idea of Progress,* (New York: Basic, 1979), 354.

PART 2

Finding Our Roots

CHAPTER 7

America and Christianity in the Beginning

It must never be forgotten that religion gave birth to Anglo-American society. In the United States, religion is therefore mingled with all the habits of the nation and all the feelings of patriotism, whence it derives a peculiar force. . . .

De Tocqueville

We have been using quotations from De Tocqueville, who wrote in 1831, to begin each chapter. Much of the American character we know today was formed by then, but what happened before that? How did a mixture of religion and political freedom combine to make us what we are? What follows is a brief overview of four hundred years of history to provide a basis for understanding our roots and, hopefully, to help keep us from repeating the mistakes of history. Others have filled in the details in hundreds of well-researched volumes.[1]

THE HISTORICAL ACCIDENT

Americans often look at "lesser developed" countries and wonder what is wrong with them. Why can't they make it? After all, *we* did. Or did we? Perhaps America was a historical accident, one that cannot be duplicated.

Up until the early sixteen hundreds North America was largely untouched by foreign settlement. Then, in the brief space of sixty years, the eastern seaboard became a series of prospering English colonies. A number of situations converged to shape a peculiarly American society.

First, the early settlers were generally superior in intelligence, determination, and ambition. Most came to America because they wanted to come, not because they were forced to come. They were not slaves who had been sent to another country, nor had the majority of them been driven out of their countries as undesirable citizens. They were people who chose to leave their homeland. They were adventurous and, for the most part, had a supreme confidence in God's guiding hand. More noticeably, they were *Protestants*, children of the Reformation, a reformation that was still very much in progress.[2]

These protesters, these reformers, had captured a new sense of what it meant to be a Christian. They sensed they had *found* that for which we look today. As a religious movement, the Reformation had a fresh insistence on the sovereignty and initiative of God. These men and women experienced what the institutionalized church they were leaving recognized only as an abstract idea. God was among them! The kingdom of God *had* arrived, even as it was yet to come. Men and women had direct access to God. He was the sole ruler. No longer was it necessary for them to contend with a series of intermediaries—priests, bishops, cardinals, popes. God was the one to whom they were directly and ultimately responsible.

We see, therefore, that Protestant Christianity was at the heart of the development of American culture and American values, and we Americans are part of the outcome. Calvin summed it up in his *Institutes:*

> We are not our own; therefore neither is our own reason or will to rule our acts and counsels. We are not our own; therefore, let us not make it our end to seek what may be agreeable to our carnal nature. We are not our own; therefore, as far as possible, let us forget ourselves and the things that are ours. On the other hand, we are God's; let us, therefore, live and die to Him (Romans XIV.8). We are

God's; therefore, let His wisdom and will preside over all our actions. We are God's; to Him, then, the only legitimate end, let every part of our life be directed.[3]

Certainly Calvin summed up the sentiments we long to live out today.

Second, although some settlers before the middle of the eighteenth century were French and Dutch, *most were English.* They spoke one language, which, in itself, became a unifying force, and had one cultural heritage. They came to the New World, but they named it after the old: *New* England, *New* York, *New* Jersey, *New* Brunswick.

Third, these American settlers were backed by an English empire that was rapidly expanding and had a great deal of capital to risk. The backers of the first Virginia settlers were called "Adventurers."[4] Today's multinational corporations might have felt comfortable with them!

Fourth, the abundance of land and natural resources in America, coupled with shortage of labor, quickly eliminated the possibility of importing Europe's feudal system with its aristocratic privileges. The alternative system, private ownership, encouraged individualism and independence. Indeed, survival depended on both these qualities. Eventually this system proved to be fertile soil for the importation of forced labor—slaves.

Fifth, although significant strides had been made in shipbuilding and in the art of navigation (without which settlement in the New World would have been impossible), the vast distance between the two countries left the administration of the new settlements very much in the hands of the settlers themselves. This, combined with the laissez-faire attitude of an English government that was concerned with its own internal struggles, gave the colonies a sense of being their own masters.[5]

These factors combined to make the early foreign settlement (the Indians might have called it "invasion") of America a very special situation. It wasn't planned. It just happened. A historical accident. Or, if you believe as did the early Reformers, God's sovereign plan. But it is the religious situation that demands our attention, for much of the American value system was shaped by religious values. To understand the genesis of these values we need to understand the impact of the Reformation on both society and on the individual.

THE NEW IDEA—THE INDIVIDUAL

Prior to the Reformation, which we usually associate with Luther's posting of his Ninety-Five Theses on the church door at Wittenberg in 1517, Christian thinking was dominated by an understanding that God's intention was to bring all humankind under His authority and that His instrument to accomplish this was the church. The church was the mediator between God and people. As such, it had the right and responsibility to control all affairs of men and women. Governments were instituted to carry out the will of God and therefore the will of the church. The church was not only holy and Roman, it headed a Holy Roman *Empire.* All men and women were expected to belong to the church, for it was the dispenser of God's grace and wisdom. In practice it sometimes compromised the lofty goals to which it aspired (it was, after all, ruled by fallible men); but it, and only it, mediated between God and individuals. It offered the sacraments, the means of grace. It offered fellowship and sanctuary. It had the ability and the power to open the gates of heaven. It was the vice-regent of the kingdom of God.

Into this environment, like a streak of summer lightning, flashed a new, revolutionary idea: Salvation was achieved only through individual faith in Jesus Christ, the only mediator between God and men. No longer did the church stand between humanity and its Creator. Salvation was viewed as an individual experience; each person must stand alone before God.

There were variations on this idea. Calvin believed the eternal destiny of each individual had been decided before the foundation of the world. And although no one could be certain if he or she was one of the elect, obedience to God demanded that one *act* as though one were. Luther believed that the choice lay with the individual, but that salvation was a matter of faith, not works. Both of these Reformation theologians placed the emphasis on the individual. How one worshipped was not the determining factor in salvation, for no ritual would satisfy God. Neither were deeds of charity the determining factor. Salvation was ultimately determined by faith or election.

The times were marked by an intense concern for one's ultimate and personal salvation. In many ways, nothing else mattered. In John Bunyan's *Pilgrim's Progress*, Pilgrim set off for the Celestial City even though his wife and children pleaded with him to stay with them. Only after he had secured his own salvation did he give thought to the eternal destiny of those he had left behind.

THREE VIEWS OF CHURCH AND STATE

Having touched briefly on the roots of individualism, we need to understand something of the historical relationship of church and state.

Americans believe in something we call the separation of church and state. When asked to define what we mean by this, however, we may have a number of different views. The Supreme Court is continually faced with new legal questions that center on this doctrine.

Prior to the Reformation at the beginning of the seventeenth century, all Christian nations saw themselves as combining within themselves both church and state. Each nation and national church were a part of the whole. Offices and functions were different, but earthly rulers held their positions by divine permission.

A feature of the state church was that all citizens of a country were assumed to be members of the church. Children were baptized as citizens of the state and as members of the family of God. Christianity was not primarily an experience; it was a body of truth to be enforced, with the help of the state if necessary.

The American idea of the need for separation between church and state came about as the result of three different reforming views.

The ideas of Luther and Calvin had spread to England at a time when England was in its own political struggle to free itself from the Church of Rome. Elizabeth had constituted herself head of the Church of England; so even though the church was no longer Roman, it was still a state church.

In the midst of these struggles were English Separatists who felt that no organic relationship between church and state should be allowed to exist. They believed the church was a gathered fellowship of true believers, and they wanted to separate the church from the state. Roger Williams, founder of the Rhode Island community, was driven out of Massachusetts (1631) because he insisted on such a separation. Separatists came from the left wing of the Reformation (Anabaptists) and out of the left wing of Puritanism (Baptists and Quakers).

One large group of churchmen was willing to recognize a state church but was persuaded that the rituals and prayer book of the Church of England had no place in Christian life. These individuals wanted to purify the church of such additions and were quickly dubbed "Puritans." From this group of Puritan dissenters came the majority of early settlers to Virginia (1607), to Plymouth (1620), and to Massachusetts Bay (1629). These Puritans did not seek to remove themselves from the church; they sought to correct it. (Unfortunately "puritan" has come to mean something quite different from the original meaning!)

In between the Separatists and the Puritans was the "middle way" of the Puritans of the Mayflower Compact (1620). They saw the visible church as a particular congregation (hence Congregationalism) made up of true believers who convenanted together to form a church whose only head was Jesus Christ. But this did not mean that such a local church could not combine with a local community to enforce its rules on that community.

The Congregationalists understood that men were still evil, and so they attempted to design both a form of worship and a form of government that would bring everyone into conformity with God's will.

> The kingdom of God was not something to be built or established nor something that came into the world from without; it was rather the rule which, having been established from eternity, needed to be obeyed despite the rebellion against it which flourished in the world. . . . To think of (the early American settlers) as primarily protesters and rebels is to regard them from a point of view foreign to their own. The first thing in their minds was positive. They were non-conformists, dissenters, protesters, independents, only because they desired to be loyal to the government of God, and in that positive allegiance they were united however much their unity was obscured for later times by their party quarrels.[6]

Thus the relationship between church and state was a foundation stone for American culture and values.

IN THE WORLD, BUT APART

The tension that continually faced these early Christians, as it faces us now, was how to be *in* the world but not *of* the world. Their tendency on one hand was to escape the corruption of the world by isolating themselves from it. On the other hand, the temptation to be a part of the world threatened to contaminate holiness. The tension between these two positions was and is crucial to Christianity. The moment we "solve" the dilemma by retreating into monasticism or by abandoning our attempts at holiness, we cease to be salt and light in the world.

H. Richard Niebuhr points to three basic components of this early American Protestantism: First, *Christian constitutionalism*, the principle that since God is the source of all power and value, His nature and His will—rather than human nature and human desires or ideals—need to be consulted in all human actions; second, the principle of *dependence of the church on God's kingdom* or, the independence of the church from earthly powers, or anything that was less than God; third, the principle of *limitation of all human power,* whether it be civil power or the power of persons within the organized church. The result, in its essence, was a democracy subject to the kingdom of God.[7]

According to Sidney E. Mead in an article entitled "The Nation With the Soul of a Church," "This development, this inversion in the conceptual order, laid the foundation for modern democracy—the idea that sovereignty, the power of God for the creation of order in communities, lies in 'the people.' It is delegated by them to rulers responsible to them."[8]

What we have seen so far is an early America peopled by men and women who saw themselves as individuals, alone before God, but who, at the same time, were members of churches that were seeking to discover God's will for the people and to legislate ways to impose this will. They were continuously searching for balance between inner feeling and rational self-control.

CHRISTIAN CALLING

Into this setting the idea of Christian calling was introduced.[9] Whereas modern translators interpret such passages as 1 Corinthians 7 as describing our status, Luther and his contemporaries believed these passages implied that a person should follow a specific vocation, or *calling.* Each individual had a task to perform in society, and that task was to be carried out with diligence and industry, not to enhance the worker but to bring honor to God. A test of Christianity was not only how one dealt with others, but how one went about one's task, one's business. But as is so often the case, an idea can be carried to an extreme. Such industriousness became a mark of high esteem to the extent that in 1695 Cotton Mather, a noted Puritan minister, declared,

> Would a Man *Rise* by his Business? I say, then, let him *Rise* to his Business. It was foretold (Proverbs 22:29), *Seest thou a man Diligent in his Business? He shall stand before Kings.* . . . Yea, how can you ordinarily enjoy any rest at Night, if you have not been well at work in the Day? Let your Business *engross* the most of your time.[10]

Such industriousness was assumed by John Wesley to be a mark of a Christian. And even though he deplored what he thought would be the eventual result, he assumed that to be a Christian was to be industrious.

> I do not see how it is possible, in the nature of things, for any revival of true religion to continue long. For religion must necessarily produce both industry and frugality, and these cannot but produce riches. But as riches increase, so will pride, anger, and love of the world in all its branches. How then is it possible that Methodism, that is, a religion of the heart, though it flourishes now as a green tree, should continue in this state? For the Methodists in every place grow diligent and frugal; consequently they increase in goods. Hence they proportionately increase in pride, in anger, in the desire of the flesh, the desire of the eyes, and the pride of life. So, although the form of religion remains, the spirit is swiftly vanishing away. Is there no way to prevent this—this continual decay of pure religion? We ought not to prevent people from being diligent and frugal; we must exhort all Christians to gain all they can, and to save all they can; that is, in effect, to grow rich.[11]

UNLIMITED WEALTH

Another notion loose in early America, though not a religious idea, combined with the Protestant work ethic in a special way. Capitalism, the idea that wealth is produced, distributed, and exchanged by private citizens rather than corporately or by the state, was a perfect companion for the Christian concept of industriousness. Max Weber has argued forcefully that this sense of calling to work itself, which lies at the heart of the "Protestant work ethic," was the genesis of the spirit of capitalism. In Weber's view, capitalism succeeds only when people are willing to accumulate wealth beyond their immediate needs, with accumulation being an end in itself.[12]

The intent of capitalism is to produce a surplus that can be used to generate additional surplus. But if this surplus is to be available to anyone willing to work, the belief in capitalism must be accompanied by a belief in unlimited wealth. America, a land of seemingly limitless abundance, appeared to be the ideal place for this philosophy to work. If wealth was available to all who would work for it, then each person could become something better. And the settlers' ability to survive in the New World indicated they were able to better their lot by finding and utilizing resources they did not have in the Old World.

And so they discovered it was possible for an individual to *change*. Previous class distinctions quickly broke down. People survived not on the basis of their station in life, but on their own ability to endure the early hardships and eventually take advantage of the natural resources they found. Instead of believing that men were created unequal, born into different classes, it became "self-evident" to the new Americans that all men were created equal, as the constitution of the new nation later stated. In other words, all Americans had an opportunity to become whatever they were able to make of themselves. Wealth was available to those willing to work for it. Instead of seeing themselves as part of a social class, the new Americans were encouraged to see themselves as having the capabilities to do all they wanted to do. The key to success lay within each individual.

Of course, luck had its part to play. The later Horatio Alger stories were always a mixture of luck and hard work. But the philosophy "Anyone can become president in America" had been born and would live on.

COMPETITION

Competition in European societies was socially unacceptable, but in the New World, individualism combined with unlimited wealth permitted competition, which came to be a hallmark of American values. Individuals could compete against one another to obtain more wealth because when one obtained more wealth it did not mean the other was losing wealth. It only meant that one had tried harder than the other (or had had better luck or had been more richly blessed).

Therefore, in a relatively short period of time—less than a century—a whole new culture was shaped, and because of its isolation from the Old World, this new culture was free to develop on its own.

FREEDOM

By the end of the seventeenth century the initial shaping force of Christianity with its concept of a kingdom society was dying, but the values of individualism, industry, and independence remained. In the midst of all this a concept of freedom—freedom to be an individual, freedom to govern own's own affairs, and, interestingly, freedom of religion—began to develop. As we have seen, although seventeenth century Americans were predominantly English, they had a wide range of beliefs about what constituted the church. But in this new situation other forces kept them from fighting over them.

The Anglicans of Virginia needed laborers and welcomed any who would come. Roger William's colony of Rhode Island was for separatists and dissenters. So how could they deny those whose beliefs were from another school of thought? The Puritans of Massachusetts had baptized their children on the strength of their own personal faith and experience. They fully expected that when their children came of age they too would have the same inner experience. But when the time came to baptize the *grandchildren*, the original settlers discovered that many of their children could *not* testify to having had a personal experience with the Lord. How then could the grandchildren be baptized on the strength of their parents' experience? The result was a compromise which came to be known as the Halfway Covenant. Individuals could continue as members of the church on the basis of Jehovah's covenant with Abraham (Gen. 17:7), even though they could not testify to a personal experiential faith.

These circumstances forced all these groups to accept a religious pluralism, which went hand in hand with the notion of religious "freedom."

At the same time a new flood of non-English immigrants was filling the land. In 1690 the total population was 200,000. By 1715 it was 400,000, including 58,850 black slaves. Other immigrants arrived. Germans and Scotch-Irish settled around the fringe of Pennsylvania, along with smaller numbers of Scotch Highlanders, French Huguenots, and those from Switzerland, Sweden, and Wales.

The forces of change continued to build, forces that could make America a completely secular society. The drives of competition and individualism threatened to completely engulf the earlier idea that individuals were to work for God's honor and that wealth was a trust over which individuals were to exercise Christian stewardship.

NOTES

[1]See George Marsden, *Fundamentalism and American Culture: The Shaping of Twentieth Century Evangelicalism—1870–1925* (New York: Oxford University Press, 1980), for a good discussion on the interplay between culture and fundamentalism.

[2]As a result of England's struggles with Roman Catholicism and Roman Catholic countries, being Roman Catholic was considered almost antipatriotic.

[3]John Calvin, *Institutes to the Christian Religion*, Book III, Ch. 7, i, Henry Beveridge, tr., 1964.

[4]Robert L. Heilbroner and Aaron Singer, *The Economic Transformation of America* (New York: Harcourt Brace Jovanovich, 1977), 13.

[5] The attempts of the crown to force a common religion on England led to the establishment of an English Protestant Commonwealth in 1640, which remained until the Restoration in 1660.

[6]H. Richard Niebuhr, *The Kingdom of God in America* (New York: Harper and Row, 1937), 56.

[7]See Niebuhr, *The Kingdom of God in America*.

[8]Sidney E. Mead, "The Nation With the Soul of a Church," *American Civil Religion*, Russell E. Richey and Donald G. Jones, eds. (New York: Harper and Row, 1974), 51.

[9]Max Weber, *Protestant Ethic and the Spirit of Capitalism*, rev. ed. (New York: Scribner, 1977), 79.

[10]Quoted from Cotton Mather's "Two Brief Discourses," Robert L. Heilbroner and Aaron Singer, *The Economic Transformation of America* (New York: Harcourt, Brace, Jovanovich, 1977), 13.

[11]Weber quotes John Wesley in *The Protestant Ethic and the Spirit of Capitalism*, 175.

[12]See Weber, *The Protestant Ethic and Spirit of Capitalism*.

CHAPTER 8 **The Making of a Civil Religion**

In the United States, Christian sects are infinitely diversified and perpetually modified; but Christianity itself is an established and irresistible fact, which no one undertakes either to attack or to defend. De Tocqueville

The first European settlers came with strong motivations to establish a new, basically religious society. They came with well-set religious convictions about what should be, what could be. In front of them lay what appeared to be unlimited opportunities for personal gain. However, few, if any, of them thought about how radically their environment would change their attitudes about wealth, about success, and about their position in life. Following close on their heels from the Continent came the humanism of the Enlightenment. In a matter of two or three generations, the dream of establishing the kingdom of God was forgotten by most. By the beginning of the eighteenth century, America might have appeared to many to be a completely secularized society.

THE GREAT AWAKENING

Just when it appeared that Christianity in America was a lost cause, the Holy Spirit intervened in such spectacular ways that the resulting phenomenon became known as the Great Awakening. Beginning in New Jersey in 1720, religious revival spread throughout the colonies. All over America people were miraculously experiencing a mighty overcoming of the Spirit. Evidences that God was in their midst were everywhere. Salvation was at hand. The kingdom of God was at hand. Could this be the long-anticipated millennium? Jonathan Edwards, the great revivalist, commented:

> It is not unlikely that this work of God's Spirit, so extraordinary and wonderful, is the dawning, or at least a prelude of the glorious work of God, so often foretold in the Scripture, which in the progress and issue of it, shall renew the work of mankind. . . . We cannot reasonably think otherwise, than that the beginning of this great work of God must be near. That there are many things that make it probable that this work will begin in America.[1]

Carried out by mass revivals and itinerant evangelists, the Great Awakening set the tone of evangelism in America for the next two hundred years. George Whitefield, Jonathan Edwards, Gilbert Tennet, and others saw tremendous results from their preaching as the awakening spread. Churches of all stripes were awakened to evangelize their neighbor. Missions to the Indians were begun anew. Philanthropic and humanitarian enterprises flourished, and Christianity became a religion of the people. The supreme test of faith was not church membership but an individual's testimony to a new birth. It elevated men and women by giving them a self-authenticating religious experience independent of clergy or church and, in so doing, strengthened the division of church and state.

THE ENLIGHTENMENT

Coincident with the Great Awakening was the Enlightenment, which was the logical result of the thinking of the English scientist Isaac Newton and the philosopher John Locke. As the Great Awakening appealed to emotions and inner feelings, the religion of the Enlightenment appealed to rational thought. "Reason" and "natural religion" became the words of the day. The new science ("natural philosophy") had different results in different people. Some used Locke and Newton to bolster their Christian orthodoxy, others to undergird their liberalism. Most, however, continued to think of themselves as Christians. Of the noted rationalists of the day, perhaps only Benjamin Franklin went all the way to deism.

Rationalism had two major aspects: first, the metaphysical oneness of the Deity (rationalism had no room for the doctrine of the Trinity); and second, the benevolent nature of God. God was good, and His goodness made the doctrine of election unthinkable, as was the horrible idea of God damning people. Original sin was repudiated. Humanity had within its power the ability to control its destiny. Although the Bible was divine revelation, it had to be validated by human reason. Ultimately all would be saved because God could never be happy as long as one person was in hell.

The rationalism of the Enlightenment found a seedbed in American culture, where pragmatic solutions dominated everyday life. The American penchant for cause and effect—"Why did this happen?"—can be traced to the Enlightenment.

To a large extent, John Locke was the philosopher who tipped the balance from the concept that human industry was designed to glorify God to the concept that industry was an activity whose end result was production and consumption. In Locke's view, people's needs and their aspirations all should be centered on the pursuit of material self interest.[2]

THE SEEDS OF REVOLUTION

During the same time, the pressures of political control from the mother country were becoming intolerable to colonists, who had become used to governing themselves through their own legislative process. In order to keep the colonies as a source of raw material and at the same time keep them from competing in areas of manufacturing, England levied a series of taxes on them to try to control commerce. The colonies reacted strongly. They were well prepared to deal with their mother country. The Great Awakening had produced a new emphasis on education; new colleges and universities had been founded. An extensive series of roads had been built; travel was easier. Weekly newspapers had become common in almost every town; communication was enhanced. All these made it possible for the thirteen sometimes desperate colonies to take concerted action against England. The result was the American Revolution.

The Declaration of Independence, which first drew the colonies together in 1776, and the Constitution, which finally established America's future course in 1789, are both pregnant with the language of the Enlightenment. Today's Christians like to project evangelical Christianity back into history, but when our founding fathers stated it was "self-evident" that "all men are created equal," their argument was based on rationalism, not on the Bible. The men who gathered to write the Constitution for the United States in Philadelphia were more children of the developing Age of Reason than they were ancestors of evangelical Christianity. Their religion began and ended in their belief that the society they were trying to create was part of an ordered universe designed by a sovereign deity. According to Thomas Howard, "If any of them were Christian, that point of view did not find expression in the national blueprint. It was a secular political entity that they fashioned."[3]

THE CONSTITUTION

Specific religious notions were involved in the framing of the Consititution, such as these in the words of Benjamin Franklin: "The existence of the Diety; that he made the world, and govern'd it by His Providence; that the most acceptable service of God was the doing of good to men;

that our souls are immortal; and that all crime will be punished, and virtue rewarded, either here or hereafter."[4] Sidney Mead points out that a century later, in 1885, these notions were so much a part of the American ethos that Josiah Strong, a congregational pastor and leader, probably thought he was merely repeating a truism when he said, "The teaching of the three great fundamental doctrines which are common to all monotheistic religions is essential to the perpetuity of free institutions, while the invocation of sectarian dogmas is not. These three doctrines are that of the *existence of God,* the *immortality of men,* and *man's accountability.*"[5]

The resulting civil religion[6] was based on these three fundamentals, which were assumed to be a part of all that was America. Although denomination piled upon denomination, until quite recently all people assumed America was "Christian" in the sense that all its citizens believed in these three principles. As we will see, the beliefs of the majority of these "Christians" varied from what we today would call "liberal" to "evangelical." But the beliefs that America was unique and that it was a gift from God remained, leading many religious leaders to believe America was responsible not only to evangelize the world but also to see that the world remained an orderly place, where the "inalienable right" of all human beings to pursue their own happiness was paramount.

Men were still living at the dawn of the coming kingdom, but, according to Niebuhr,

> It was secularized by being detached from its context of faith in the sovereignty and of the experience of grace, while it was attached to the idea of human sovereignty and natural freedom. It was nationalized, being used to support the feeling of national superiority and of manifest destiny. It was confused with the progress of industrialism and capitalism. It was conceived in tragically literal fashion by the Bill of Rights. It was used to justify war and violence in the days of the English crisis. But even these abnormal forms of hope indicated the power it had over the minds of

American Christians. To an ever increasing extent they turned from the expectation of heavenly bliss to the hope of a radical transformation of life upon earth, without abandoning the former as though the two expectations were exclusive of each other.[7]

INSTITUTIONALIZING THE KINGDOM

The doctrine of the kingdom of God, which had been built by the first Americans, had within it the seeds of its own destruction. On the one hand it looked upon the individual as the basic unit of society. It was the individual who stood alone before an awesome God and trusted life to Him. On the other hand, the kingdom as the rule of God called all men and women to be subject to God's rule and to see themselves as stewards of God's creation, to work for the good of that creation. The freedom of the individual triumphed over the responsibility to God for society. Man took his destiny back from God.

The idea of the kingdom was not abandoned, however. As often happens, the words were given new meaning. The kingdom became the rule of law, rather than the rule of Christ. It became institutionalized, an end in itself. It became infected by humanism and a belief that man was the ultimate shaper of his own destiny.

And did not God's Word say that man was to have dominion over creation and all its resources? The very abundance of natural resources in America led American Christians to interpret certain passages of Scripture to mean that it was man's responsibility to use them. And, since there seemed to be unlimited natural resources, people did not think they were exploiting those resources. Consequently, the blessed land of America became more important than the kingdom.

YANKEE INGENUITY AND INTERCHANGEABLE PARTS

The task of using the resources at hand led to a continuous search for new ways to use them. "Yankee ingenuity" developed. Thousands of individuals invented new ways of obtaining more resources in less time, thereby accumulating wealth. Technology and the domination of the environment became major themes in American thinking. The West was to be "conquered." The land was to be "tamed." Man was at war with nature, and the titanic struggle was viewed as a great challenge. Part of this conquest involved raw materials, but much of it involved new ways of manufacturing things. The introduction of interchangeable parts significantly colored American thinking. Up until the mid-1800s many things looked alike, but few manufactured goods were interchangeable with one another. In other words, if a wagon lost a wheel, a new one had to be specially made to fit the old axle. But with the introduction of interchangeable parts, a whole new era of technology developed.

Although the idea of interchangeable parts dates back to the late 1700s, and although technology for it was first developed in France and Britain, the concept was first utilized on a large scale by Eli Whitney, the American inventor of the cotton gin, in the manufacture of rifles in the very early 1800s.

The "American System" as it was soon called, was not instantaneously successful. It would not be until the general technology of machine-tool production made the task of creating multiples a simple rather than a demanding one: As late as 1824 it was considered a feat when the Harper's Ferry arsenal produced muskets with interchangeable bayonets. In 1815 the new technique was applied to the manufacturing of wooden clocks, and Eli and Seth Thomas began to assemble 500 wooden clocks at a single time. Thereafter Chauncy Jerome applied the idea to brass clocks; then in 1846 it was used in making of sewing machines; in 1847 for farm machinery; in 1848, for watch parts; in 1853, for the famous Colt revolver.[8]

This new concept not only permitted people to utilize natural resources more effectively—accomplish more in less time—but it also led to the application of the idea of interchangeable parts to human organization. Today it is not uncommon for organizations to write "position descriptions" describing the type of person needed to fit a particular block on the organization chart. If one individual will not fit, another will be found who will.

If evidence was needed that man had taken charge of the world, this was it. American Christians may have talked about the kingdom of God, but they were really saying, "We can do it ourselves."

NOTES

[1]Jonathan Edwards, *The Works of President Edwards*, (10 volumes, New York, 1829), Volume IV,   128, as quoted in H. Richard Niebuhr, *The Kingdom of God in America* (New York: Harper and Row, 1937),   141.

[2]See John Locke, *Two Treatises of Government* (London: Cambridge University Press, 1967).

[3]Thomas Howard, "The Evangelical Christian and the American Civil Religion," *The Cross and the Flag*, Robert G. Clouse et al., eds. (Carol Stream: Creation House, 1972),   55.

[4]Russell E. Richey and Donald G. Jones, eds., *American Civil Religion* (New York: Harper and Row, 1974),   57.

[5]See Sidney E. Mead, *Lively Experiment: The Shaping of Christianity in America* (New York: Harper and Row, 1963).

[6]First use of the term *civil religion* is attributed to Robert Bellah. See his book *The Broken Covenant: American Civil Religion in Time of Trial* (New York: Seabury, 1976).

[7]Niebuhr, *The Kingdom of God in America*,   151.

[8]Robert L. Heilbroner and Aaron Singer, *The Economic Transformation of America* (New York: Harcourt Brace Jovanovich, 1977),   45.

CHAPTER 9

A New World View

> *Equality ... tends to isolate them from each other, to concentrate every man's attention upon himself; and it lays open the soul to an inordinate love of material gratification.*
>
> De Tocqueville

Changes in the secular world view were accompanied by a change in the Christian world view. By the nineteenth century the identity crisis of the kingdom of God was past. The kingdom was no longer sought because most Christians believed it had already arrived. Some thought it had been ushered in by the American Revolution, or perhaps by the birth of modern science. Others pointed to the Great Awakening or to the Protestant Reformation as the beginning of the kingdom. But to most, God's kingdom and America had been fused into one entity. Thus society, because it was mistakenly identified with Christianity, was free to shape itself.

It is important to realize here that America had not become pagan. The majority of nineteenth-century Americans would have scored very well on any contemporary test of evangelical doctrine.

Sparked in the 1850s by another awakening, the "Christianizing" of America continued and spread to other nations as well. Missionaries to "savage lands" carried the Good News to peoples around the world. In 1792 William Carey estimated that only one-third of the nations of the world had a Christian witness;[1] but by the end of the nineteenth century, almost every country of the world had some testimony to Christ within its boundaries.

The expansion of Christianity was accompanied by a widely held belief that the Millennium had begun and that Christ's second coming would follow the Millennium. Thus, Western expansionism was very easily equated with God's plan to carry the gospel to every nation, tribe, and tongue.

But a radical shift away from this postmillennial position occurred at the end of the nineteenth century. Richard Niebuhr sums it up so well that I quote him at length:

> But this vision collapsed after the Civil War and was replaced by an eschatology that looked for the return of Christ to rescue the "saints" *out of this world.* Premillennial teaching implied that the world was in such bad shape that it would only get worse until the return of Christ. Some even argued that efforts to ameliorate social conditions would merely postpone the "blessed hope" of Christ's return by delaying the process of degeneration. Premillennialism was articulated to the Evangelical world through conferences for the study of biblical prophecy that began in the 1870s and had a cumulative effect in the following decades. . . . The postwar revivalism of evangelist D.L. Moody was, for example, closely tied to this new eschatology. By the 1920s Wheaton College, originally motivated by the postmillennial vision of Jonathan Blanchard, had written premillennial doctrines into a theological platform. . . .
>
> Those conditioned to think that Evangelical theological discussions are resolved exclusively by scriptural exegesis would be astonished to discover the extent to which resolution of these eschatological issues depended upon matters of taste and perceptions of the direction in which the world was moving. Much of the appeal in the argumen-

tation was to empirical evidence. The postmillennialists pointed to the progress of foreign missions and the spread of literacy to prove that the world was in fact getting better and better. Premillennialists, on the other hand, cited the rise of crime and social problems, often primarily in the cities, as evidence that the world was growing more evil. Apparently a great deal depended on reading these "Signs of the times"!

This shift in eschatology had profound, and somewhat mixed, impact on the social involvement of Evangelicals. On the one hand, the expectation of the imminent return of Christ freed many from building for the immediate future (social advancement, pension plans, etc.) to give themselves wholeheartedly to the inner cities and foreign mission fields. Resulting contact with poor and oppressed peoples often pushed these devoted souls into relief and other welfare work—and occasionally into reform.

But more characteristic was the tendency to abandon long-range social amelioration for a massive effort to preach the gospel to as many as possible before the return of Christ. The vision was now one of rescue from a fallen world. Just as Jesus was expected momentarily on the clouds to rapture his saints, so the slum worker established missions to rescue sinners out of the world to be among those to meet the Lord in the air. Evangelical effort that had once provided the impulse and troops for reform rallies was rechanneled into exegetical speculation about the timing of Christ's return and into maintenance of the expanding prophecy conferences.[2]

It would be fair to say that by the beginning of the twentieth century the notion of progress had completely freed itself from religious control and now dominated the culture.

THE RESULTS OF PLURALISM

Pluralism and individualism, the dominant features of early American life, demanded that people be treated "equally" and be seen as having equal value. This meant that even if outward circumstances contradicted the idea that two people were equal, the social system demanded that superiors deal with inferiors as though they were equals.

The idea of equality permeated the design of American government institutions. When a new government office was created, attempts were made to ensure that all of the public with which it dealt would be treated in the same way. But treating people equally led to the idea that people were not unique. Thus bureaucrats concluded that since all people are the same, no one is really special. A self-serving bureaucracy has therefore become a feature of American life,[3] and encounters with this bureaucracy have caused many Americans to feel lonely and helpless. "What difference," we wonder "can one individual make in and against such a machine-like world?"

CULTURAL ISOLATION

American culture took on a life of its own apart from the rest of the world. Separated by vast expanses of oceans and, as we noted earlier, apparently endowed with unlimited resources, America gave its citizens little reason to look "outside." The land was large. And, through conquest and acquisition, it grew even larger. It was unified by common language. America became, in size and common purpose, something never before seen. As a result, Americans became self-centered and self-satisfied with what America was and what it had accomplished. This also led to an ignorance of other cultures and other countries, which Americans viewed as "strange."

REWRITING HISTORY

All societies tend to interpret their past in light of their present situation and understanding of life and the world. After all, we have a need to explain why we are the way we are. But those who live in a rapidly changing society, a society that emphasizes that what is new and different is better, are continually forced to rewrite history.

Of course, that is not what we are taught in school.

History is *taught* as a set of facts. "This is the way it was." True, we sometimes read, "We *now* understand what was really going on." But few school children doubt what their teachers tell them about what happened in the early settlement of America.

Frances Fitzgerald has done an excellent job of demonstrating this phenomenon in *America Revised*. As Fitzgerald reviews the history of America as seen through textbooks written for school children, she demonstrates how we have continually reinterpreted history. For example, in the early 1800s schoolroom textbooks defined the national identity as white, Protestant, and suspicious of strangers. Early American history books portrayed Indians as savages. In later texts they became "noble savages." Their role as "native Americans" has only recently been recognized.

This ability to constantly rewrite history to fit our current world view cuts us off from a sense of history and continuity and helps explain the American obsession with modern (up-to-date) science, which is assumed to supersede what was "known" before. We conclude that the last generation really didn't understand history, but that we moderns, with our greater insight and our tools of "psychohistory," are able to understand *what really happened*. Not only do we enlist new facts for a better understanding of our history, but we claim new insight, insight which (in our opinion) no one before us has had.

This ability to easily rewrite history has also cut us off from our Christian heritage. We American evangelicals seem to believe we have discovered something "new" with each turn of theological thought. We eagerly want to propagate these new revelations, these "words from the Lord," to others. We suppose that Christians of an earlier age were deprived of the scientific or modern abilities we have that enable us to see and understand. And as we have seen, this has been the situation among American evangelicals for over 150 years. What a shock it would be to most supporters of prestigious Wheaton College to know that the institution was founded by men who were postmillien-nialists to the core, and who were political activists to boot!

THE TECHNOLOGICAL FIX

The emphasis on technology goes hand in hand with American materialism. If the purpose of technology is to accumulate the natural resources of the world for our-selves, either to give us more time to do what we want to do or just for the satisfaction of possessing the actual resources, then our personal success is determined by how effectively we have used that technology. The result has been a world view that sees everything as subject to the technological fix. The continual stream of new inven-tions and new materials leads to the logical conclusion that whatever problems we face today, "science" will be able to "fix" tomorrow. The world is consequently seen as problems that need to be solved. This world view transfers itself from things to people, thus creating the American obsession with "interpersonal relationships." We even apply it to ourselves, as evidenced by the numerous how-to-do-it and self-help books that are so popular. So we see a progression of the application of technology: First, it was needed to conquer nature; second, to extract from nature what was needed; third, to design a better way of living; fourth, to design the social and organizational relation-ships of human beings; and finally, to permit the ultimate improvement of the individual by the individual—com-plete absorption with one's self.

A great deal of American education is based on the notion of the technological fix. Individuals are seen as needing skills and knowledge that will help them "suc-ceed" in life and in society. They are expected to make a contribution to society, but that contribution is secondary to personal achievement. American education thus em-phasizes how to *do*, rather than how to *be*. It ignores the transcendental and the spiritual and concerns itself with what it considers to be "real"—the material. Colleges and universities, therefore, point with pride to graduates who have made outstanding personal achievements.

CAUSE AND EFFECT

The emphasis on technology and problem solving logically leads to the emphasis on cause and effect. If we want to duplicate the successes of another, we need to know what was done. We need to know why things work, what caused a particular event. This continual probing for cause and effect, when applied to the individual, eventually leads to extreme narcissism. We keep looking inwardly for the causes (psychological and spiritual) of our situation. The result is *self*-commitment.

Other American ideas about the world have similar effects. The American concept that anyone can "make it" if he or she only tries hard enough and long enough leads Americans to deny responsibility for poverty, both in our country and in places around the world. Why should we be committed to poor people? After all, if they worked as hard as we do, they could make it too. We forget the "accident of history" that produced our country.

This emphasis on the future and on everyone's ability to eventually succeed tends to cut us off from our own history. What happened in the past is of little consequence; what we do with the *future* is our ultimate concern. As a result, we have no commitment to traditions and values of the past. Further, our emphasis on facts, rather than on concepts and ideas, keeps us from reflecting on the root causes of the social conditions in the world and keeps us from seeing how really different we are, both in our circumstances and in our resulting culture, from other peoples and countries of the world.

Richard Niebuhr believed the church was used to preserve this philosophy, which was crucial to the survival of capitalism.

> To be reconciled to God now meant to be reconciled to the established customs of a more or less Christianized

society. As the Christian church became the protector of the social mores so its revivals tended to become instruments for enforcing the prevailing standards. As it became increasingly clear how perilous the use of liquor was in the democratic and industrial society a revival was used especially to combat this evil. Men were now saved not from the frustration, conflict, futility and poverty of life which they sought to escape in the saloons; they were saved from whiskey. And the revivals were sometimes used in less evidently useful ways, to enforce the codes of capitalist industry, to overcome the rebellion of workers and to foster their bourgeois virtues on which the success of the industrial system depended.[4]

The result of this constant intertwining of the religious with the secular has produced today's civil religion. American civil religion gives the impression that we *are* in God's country. The close relationship between the idea that "this *is* a Christian nation" and our evangelical desire to *make* it a Christian nation, can lead us to believe that our desire and the facts are the same. We are still captured, though perhaps subconsciously, by the idea that the kingdom of God is ours, here and now.

THE LAST ONE HUNDRED YEARS

By the last quarter of the nineteenth century, religion no longer played a significant role in the shaping of American culture. But even after the religious force was removed, many religious values remained. Stores stayed closed on Sunday. Courtroom witnesses took the oath to be truthful with one hand on a Bible ("So help me, God"). Not to be a member of a church was socially unacceptable.

If we are going to interact with our culture, we need to understand the major shift that essentially removed these remaining religious values. What were the sources that made this cultural shift occur?

In his book *The Cultural Contradictions of Capitalism*, sociologist Daniel Bell points to mass consumption as the basic source of a major cultural transformation.

The cultural transformation of modern society is due, singularly, to the rise of mass consumption, or the diffusion of what were once considered luxuries to the middle and lower classes in society. In this process, past luxuries are constantly redefined as necessities, so that it eventually seems incredible that an ordinary object could ever have been considered out of the reach of an ordinary man. . . .

Mass consumption, which began in the 1920s, was made possible by revolutions in technology, principally the application of electrical energy to household tasks (washing machines, refrigerators, vacuum cleaners, and the like), and by three social inventions: mass production on an assembly line, which made a cheap automobile possible; the development of marketing, which rationalized the art of identifying different kinds of buying groups and whetting consumer appetites; and the spread of installment buying, which, more than any other social device, broke down the *old Protestant fear of debt* [italics mine]. The concomitant revolutions in transportation and communications laid the basis for a national society and the beginnings of a common culture. Taken all together, mass consumption meant the acceptance, in the crucial area of life-style, of the idea of social change and personal transformation, and it gave legitimacy to those who would innovate and lead the way, in culture as well as in production.[5]

Bell points to two other major factors that radically changed society: The automobile drove down the isolation of the small towns, an isolation which did much to enforce a strict moral code. And the cinema brought to Americans a picture of a world that was far different from the one experienced by most middle-class citizens.

A society in rapid change inevitably produces confusions about appropriate modes of behavior, taste, and dress. A socially mobile person has no ready guide for acquiring new knowledge on how to live "better" than before, and his guides become the movies, television, and advertising. In this respect, advertising begins to play a more subtle role in changing habits than merely stimulating wants. The advertising in the women's magazines, the house-and-home periodicals, and sophisticated journals like the *New Yorker* was to teach people how to dress, furnish a home, buy the right wines—in short, the styles of life appropriate to the new statuses. Though at first the changes were primarily in manners, dress, taste, and food habits, sooner or later they began to affect more basic patterns: the structure of authority in the family, the role of children and young adults as independent consumers in the society, the pattern of morals, and the different meanings of achievement in the society.[6]

The third social invention Bell lists is installment credit.

None of this would have been possible without the revolution in moral habit, *the idea of installment selling* [italics mine]. Although it had been practiced fitfully in the United States before World War I, installment selling had two stigmas. First, most installment sales were to the poor, who could not afford major expenditures; they paid weekly sums to a peddler who both sold the goods and made the weekly collection. Installment selling was thus a sign of financial instability. Second, installment selling meant debt to the middle class, and going into debt was wrong and dangerous.

Saving—or abstinence—is the heart of the Protestant ethic. With Adam Smith's idea of parsimony or frugality, and Nassau Senior's idea of abstinence, it was firmly established that saving multiplied future products and earned its own reward by interest. The denouement was the change in banking habits. For years, such was the grim specter of middle-class morality that people were afraid to be overdrawn at the bank, lest a check bounce. By the end of the 1960s, the banks were strenuously advertising the services of cash reserves that would allow a depositor to overdraw up to several thousand dollars (to be paid back in monthly installments). No one need be deterred from gratifying his impulse at an auction or a sale. The seduction of the consumer had become total.[7]

It is only fitting to bring this analysis of the development of American culture into the present with a closing quote from Bell:

What this abandonment of Puritanism and the Protestant ethic does, of course, is to leave capitalism with no moral or transcendental ethic. It also emphasizes not only the disjunction between the norms of the culture and the norms of the social structure, but also an extraordinary contradiction within the social structure itself. On the one hand, the business corporation wants an individual to work hard, pursue a career, accept delayed gratification—to be, in the crude sense, an organization man. And yet, in its products and its advertisements, the corporation promotes pleasure, instant joy, relaxing and letting go. One is to be "straight" by day and a "swinger" by night. This is self-fulfillment and self-realization![8]

BUT WHAT OF THE PRESENT?

Everything we have said so far could have been said in 1960. But in the minds of most Americans these past twenty years, and especially the last ten, have been particularly disturbing.

In 1831 De Tocqueville forecast a gloomy future for this young democracy. He predicted that American individualism would soon alienate American citizens from one another to such a degree that the society would no longer be able to function. Many today might not identify the same root cause, but would agree that we have lost what was at the core of all we believed in as Americans.

The critics argue over the specifics: Was it the loss of national nerve caused by the Vietnam War with all its atrocities? Is it all the self-awareness movements that surround us? Have our young people lost their commitment? In a major address in 1969 Margaret Mead, one of America's most distinguished scholars of human society, gave a series of lectures on "Culture and Commitment: A Study of the Generation Gap."[9] She stated forcefully that there was indeed a generation gap, one so broad that it defied most attempts to communicate across it. She described American youth as no longer finding anything of worth to which to give their commitment. The values of their parents seem out of place in a world compressed by instant communication that constantly describes the desperate condition of most of the rest of the inhabitants of planet earth.

Christopher Lasch says we now have a "culture of narcissism."[10] And I would contend, as I did at the beginning of this book, that we evangelical Christians are not only mightily infected with the disease of narcissism, but that it has robbed us of our ability to be the people of God against the world and yet for the world.

NOTES

[1]William Carey, *An Inquiry Into the Obligation of Christians to Use Means for the Conversion of the Heathen.* A facsimile of the 1792 edition is available from Carey Kingsgate Press, London.

[2]H. Richard Niebuhr, *The Kingdom of God in America* (New York: Harper and Row, 1937),   179–181. Also see George M. Marsden, *Fundamentalism and American Culture* (New York: Oxford University Press, 1980).

[3]See Peter L. Berger et al., *Homeless Mind: Modernization and Consciousness* (New York: Irvington, 1973).

[4]Niebuhr, *The Kingdom of God in America,*   181.

[5]Daniel C. Bell, *The Cultural Contradictions of Capitalism* (New York: Basic, 1976),   65–66.

[6]Ibid.,   69.

[7]Ibid.,   69–70.

[8]Ibid.,   71–72.

[9]See Margaret Mead, *Culture and Commitment: The New Relations Between the Generations in the 1970s* (New York: Doubleday, 1978).

[10]See Christopher Lasch, *The Culture of Narcissism: American Life in an Age of Diminishing Returns* (New York: Norton, 1979).

PART 3

Recapturing
Commitment

CHAPTER 10

How Do We Respond?

Individualism, at first, only saps the virtues of public life; but, in the long run, it attacks and destroys all others, and is at length absorbed in downright selfishness. Selfishness is a vice as old as the world, which does not belong to one form of society more than to another: individualism is of democratic origin, and it threatens to spread in the same ratio as the equality of condition. De Tocqueville

What is the difference between American society and evangelical Christian society? Not much. Are we evangelicals making a difference in the world? Not much. Some hoped the Moral Majority would bring back standards of personal and public morality. To date it doesn't look like that is going to happen.

What is the difference between the average middle-class American and the average middle-class Christian? Not much. Most of us live in neighborhoods with nice, kind, considerate families, very few of whom even know what the term evangelical means. It's often difficult to discern a Christian from any other person in the community; their homes are no different and their discussions about drug abuse are no different from those heard at most local PTA meetings. The Christian counseling profession is thriving.

When asked about aspirations, hopes, and fears, answers from evangelicals aren't much different from those of any other groups.

We have bought into something called success. We have equated spiritual blessing with material prosperity and spiritual peace with physical comfort. We want to look good, feel good, be well thought of. We want people to believe that Christians have made it! The only trouble is, we have let the world define for us what we mean by "made it."

America is suffering from a tremendous sense of loss— that numbing feeling that nothing or no one is worth being committed to. And if there is nothing worth being committed to, then there is nothing worth living for, and life is one big joke.

Built into the core of Christianity is a commitment dramatically different from anything the world or the American Dream has to offer: a commitment to a community of believers that is coupled to a commitment to our Lord and Master is what the church is *supposed* to be all about, but seldom is in America. It is a set of relationships with the potential to be so strong and secure that the world could only respond, "See how they love one another."

Where have we missed it? What is it really supposed to be like? How can we get it back again? How can we demonstrate to ourselves and to the world, our world, our America, the height and depth and breadth of God's love ?

Read with me some passages of Scripture that are familiar to many of us. Let's rehearse what God has said about us and to us.

An infinite, omnipotent, omniscient God, in ways that are too mysterious for us to understand, knew us, chose us before the foundation of the world:

> For he chose us in him before the creation of the world
> to be holy and blameless in his sight. In love he predestined
> us to be *adopted as his sons* through Jesus Christ, in

accordance with his pleasure and will—to the praise of his glorious grace, which he has freely given us in the One he loves (Eph. 1:4–6).

For those God foreknew he also predestined to be conformed to the likeness of his Son, that he might be the firstborn among many brothers. And those he predestined, he also called; those he called, he also justified; those he justified, he also glorified (Rom. 8:29–30).

The reason for this was so that we might live for God's glory:

In him we were also chosen, having been predestined according to the plan of him who works out everything in conformity with the purpose of his will, in order that we, who were the first to hope in Christ, *might be for the praise of his glory* (Eph. 1:11–12).

But we did not begin life this way. We were not born Christians. We were born as citizens of another world:

Remember that at that time you were separate from Christ, excluded from citizenship in Israel and foreigners to the covenants of promise, *without hope and without God* in the world (Eph. 2:12).

But because of what Christ has done for us, and (again mysteriously) because of the faith that we have placed in His life, death, and resurrection, we have become citizens of God's household:

Consequently, you *are no longer foreigners and aliens, but fellow citizens* with God's people and members of God's household, built on the foundation of the apostles and prophets, with Christ Jesus himself as the chief corner-stone (Eph. 2:19–20).

Notice the analogy of the household. Each one of us is part of a whole:

In Him the whole building is joined together and rises to become a holy temple in the Lord. And in him *you too are being built together* to become a dwelling in which God lives by his Spirit (Eph. 2:21–22).

Once you were alienated from God and *were enemies in your minds* because of your evil behavior. But now he has reconciled you by Christ's physical body through death to present you holy in his sight, without blemish and free from accusation—if you continue in your faith, established and firm, not moved from the hope held out in the gospel (Col. 1:21–23).

For he has rescued us from the dominion of darkness and brought us into the kingdom of the Son he loves, in whom we have redemption, the forgiveness of sins (Col. 1:13–14).

When we are called out of the world, we are called into a new relationship, a relationship Paul could only describe as a mystery, a concept with which evangelicals struggle:

Just as each of us has one body with many members, and these members do not all have the same function, so in Christ we who are many form one body, and each member *belongs to all the others* (Rom. 12:5).

This is Christ's body. Christ is the head of the church, his body, of which he is Savior.

Humanly speaking, we were individuals before we were brought into this body, but now we are no longer individuals. In the same way that an arm cannot exist without an elbow and a circulatory system, we cannot exist without other members of this body. We may still be seen as individual parts of the body, but in truth we cannot live this life apart from one another.

We have different gifts, according to the grace given us. If a man's gift is prophesying, let him use it in proportion to his faith. If it is serving, let him serve; if it is teaching, let him teach; if it is encouraging, let him encourage; if it is contributing to the needs of others, let him give generously; if it is leadership, let him govern diligently; if it is showing mercy, let him do it cheerfully (Rom. 12:6–8).

These gifts are given to each one and they are given for the common good.

Now to each one the manifestation of the Spirit is given *for the common good.* To one there is given through the Spirit the message of wisdom, to another the message of knowledge by means of the same Spirit, to another faith by the same Spirit, to another gifts of healing by that one Spirit, to another miraculous powers, to another prophecy, to another the ability to speak in different kinds of tongues, and to still another the interpretation of tongues. All these are the work of one and the same Spirit, and he gives them to each man, just as he determines (1 Cor. 12:7–11).

And as Paul so beautifully points out in the balance of the twelfth chapter of Corinthians, "the body is not made up of one part but of many," and "God has arranged the parts in the body, every one of them, just as he wanted them to be. . . . God has combined the members of the body and has given greater honor to the parts that lacked it, so that there should be no division in the body, but that its parts should have equal concern for each other."

Let's not miss the key idea here: "If one part suffers, every part suffers with it; if one part is honored, every part rejoices with it" (1 Cor. 12:26).

Are there individuals then in this body? Of course. Each individual is gifted. Each is a part, a describable part—a foot, an eye, an arm. But there is no room for individual*ism*. The "self" is no longer *me*, but *us*. And the primary concern of the Lord for this body is that it should be "built up." In fact, this is the primary reason these different gifts are given:

It was he who gave some to be apostles, some to be prophets, some to be evangelists, and some to be pastors and teachers, to prepare God's people for works of service, *so that the body of Christ may be built up* until we all reach unity in the faith and in the knowledge of the Son of God and become mature, attaining to the whole measure of the fullness of Christ. . . . From him the whole body, joined and held together by every supporting ligament, grows and builds itself up in love, as each part does its work (Eph. 4:11–13).

Even the gift of evangelist is given so that the body may be built up. And as the body is built, obviously so are the parts of the body. How ridiculous for us to say that we are in a program of exercise and diet to build up our body but that we have no concern for our hands or arms or legs. Weak arms are the product of a weak body. Tired muscles are part of a tired body.

Do we want to be built up as Christians? Build the body. Give your life to the Head and His Body so that you may have life more abundantly.

THREE LEVELS OF COMMITMENT

What we see from this are three levels of commitment.[1] Each is part of the other; each is part of the whole.

Certainly our primary commitment is to the person of God in Christ. To Him and to Him only we owe allegiance. This commitment, this relationship, transcends all other commitments, even the "one-flesh" commitment to our spouse. If a person wants to follow Jesus, he or she must be willing to leave father and mother, sister and brother and to put all previous commitments aside. The difference between Christianity and other religions is commitment to a *Person* who is God!

Christianity is more than a commitment to a relationship. It is a willingness to sacrifice all of life for that person or that group of people. How glibly we wear crosses in our lapels and hang them from golden chains worn around our necks. Perhaps we could better capture the true meaning of that cross if it were a guillotine or a hangman's noose. Then the testimony of that cross would be a testimony to our willingness to be executed for the sake of Christ. Think for a moment about this analogy. The cross is a testimony that we have died to the "old self," a self of individualism. We have been raised up from death by the power of and under the control of God's spirit, but the life we now live is not our own. It belongs to Christ, and more particularly, in its earthly existence, it belongs to His body, the church. Not only are we incomplete outside the body, but the body is incomplete without us. We are fitted together in a special way. Our particular talents and capabilities and gifts are needed to make up the whole. To be in Christ is to be in His body.

Therefore, once the first commitment to God in Christ is made, the second level of commitment must follow. But that's not how most American Christians think. Our individualism, combined with our activism, suggests that as soon as we have made the first commitment, we must strike out immediately to *serve* Christ. "I am *yours*, Lord! I am ready to go. What is it you want me to *do*?"

The answer is disconcerting. "Right now I don't want you to *do* anything. I want you to understand who you are. I want you to *be*. I want you to be a part of my body, my church." And this is the second commitment we have when we come to Christ, a commitment to the church.

This church, although it is the church universal, is not an abstract fraternity or an association. Rather, it is local, parochial, and present here and now. It is made up of a *local* body of believers. It is like a vine that sends its roots under the ground and then flowers in one particular place. The church is somehow, in a way that is difficult to comprehend or even to model, all connected. But we are gifted and fitted at any given moment in history to be part of some *local* community.

What a fantastic truth! At the moment of conversion, at the moment I accepted Christ, the Holy Spirit was given to me as a guarantee of my inheritance in the future—at that moment God had prepared a place, a role, for me as a working part of a local fellowship! And just as importantly, I am *needed*. The church is not complete without me. A local fellowship has been especially prepared for each one of us, and we have been especially prepared to make the church complete wherever we are. Some of us may be capable of great physical exploits, some may be paraplegics, but we all are needed. The values of this fellowship are upside down compared to those of the world. Those who are the "least gifted" can rejoice! They are to be honored:

> On the contrary, those parts of the body that *seem to be weaker are indispensable,* and the parts that we think are less honorable we treat with special honor. And the parts that are unpresentable are treated with special modesty, while our presentable parts need no special treatment. But God has combined the members of the body and has given *greater* honor to the parts that lacked it, so that there should be no division in the body, but that its parts should have equal concern for each other (1 Cor. 12:22–25).

COMMITMENT TO SELF

This is all backward from what we are learning from our culture, which is telling us that our first commitment must be to ourselves—*Numero Uno.* God's Word comes at it from a different viewpoint.

> For by the grace given me I say to everyone of you: Do not think of yourself more highly than you ought, but rather *think of yourself with sober judgment,* in accordance with the measure of faith God has given you. . . . Live in harmony with one another. Do not be proud, but be willing to associate with people of low position. Do not be conceited (Rom. 12:3, 16).

> If you have any encouragement from being united with Christ, if any comfort from his love, if any fellowship with the Spirit, if any tenderness and compassion, then make my joy complete by being *like-minded,* having the *same love,* being *one* in *spirit and purpose.* Do nothing out of selfish ambition or vain conceit, but in humility consider others better than yourselves. Each of you should look not only to your own interests, but also to the interests of others (Phil. 2:1–4).

In addition to our commitment to Christ, then, we are called on to make a second commitment at the moment of our new birth in Christ. It is a commitment to a local group of Christians within whom dwells all the power of Christ.

But what about the work of Christ? If the first level of our commitment is given to Christ, and the second, our commitment to a local fellowship and to one another, flows naturally from it, how does the work get done? This question brings us to the third level of commitment.

The work of Christ is the work of Christ's church, not the work of individuals. From the world's view the work may appear to be carried out by individuals, but the life-support system of these individuals is intimately connected with the body of which they are a part. This work is carried on both within and without the local fellowship. The body is to be built up. Individual parts are to be strengthened and encouraged. We are to grow up into Christ. But there is also a task to be done outside the church, in the society, in the culture. The question of our response to our culture is therefore a question to be answered by a local assembly of believers.

This local church is unlike any other association. Set before it are two seemingly irreconcilable tasks. On the one hand, it is to build up the sick, the weak, and the downtrodden in its midst. On the other hand, it is to go forth into the world. In the words of Elizabeth O'Connor, the church must be constantly on a journey inward and a journey outward.[2]

The picture of the early church in the book of Acts gives us an idea of how proper commitment causes Christians to operate for the good of one another. The "work" the early Christians did was the natural outpouring of love they had for their risen Lord and for one another. There was freedom. There was spontaneity. The sick were cared for. Widows were helped. Goods were shared. The good news of the kingdom was proclaimed both in Jerusalem and in Judea and to the ends of the earth. How can we describe them? Perhaps "See how they love one another" says it all.

THE LOCAL CHURCH TODAY

But what of our local assemblies today? What are they like?

Let me contrast this picture of the early church with a picture of a typical modern-day evangelical church. Imagine what visitors to your church might experience on any given Sunday morning. Walk with them to your church service. Read the bulletin with its various listings. Listen to the sermon. Walk among the different buildings. Notice the signs, the posters. Look at the people. Observe the cars in the parking lot. Observe people as they come to church for worship, as they (perhaps) stay for Sunday school, and as they leave. What might your visitors conclude?

For the most part, our churches look much like any American business establishment. They have organization charts, committees, structures. The listings of paid staff members and official boards indicate that churches, as well as businesses, believe in authority and power structures. Churches operate as a series of enterprises. They have mission outreaches—Sunday school, a calling program, and Boy Scouts and Girl Scouts or Pioneer Girls and Boy's Brigade.

We like statistics. We compare the number of people present this Sunday with the number present last Sunday. And visitors can see by reading the bulletin that we are concerned about the offering and the monetary contribution of our members.

Church growth is important to us. We seek to "attract new members" and to "hold onto the older ones." But attendance in our worship services seems to indicate that we accept the fact that large numbers of "committed Christians" are not members of any local church. (But I have never heard anyone wonder whether or not the absence of these unchurched Lone Rangers inhibits the rest of us from carrying out the functions of Christ's body.)

We appreciate the external trappings of wealth and well-being. The pews are comfortable (perhaps even padded),

the sanctuary is well-heated (perhaps even air conditioned), and the parking lot has plenty of room (one of the
keys to church growth is plenty of parking space).

We emphasize the importance of the individual. Having a
good preacher is on the top of the priority list, and a good
administrator is a valued person. We recruit individuals to
serve on committees, usually for a stated period of time,
and we believe individuals need to be "motivated" to
convince them to serve in the church.

We accept that the division between church and state
also includes a division between sacred and secular. The
church doesn't "meddle in politics," nor does it try to tell
its members what kind of employment they should have.
(It had better not!) This description of the church, though
somewhat negative, is not meant to imply that today's
church is all bad; rather, it is intended to point out that
instead of viewing the church as an organism that gives life
and meaning to its members, without which they cannot
survive, we view it as an institution that people join *as a
matter of personal discretion.*

TO WHAT LOCAL CHURCH AM I COMMITTED?

Members of such churches continue to act as individuals. A young Christian executive who is offered a great new
"opportunity" for advancement within his or her company
often prays about the opportunity. Indeed, he or she may
ask the local church to pray also, asking God's wisdom for
the right decision. More often than not the mutual
decision is that the individual should accept this opportunity and perhaps "have a greater testimony for Christ" in a
"higher" position.

And so a move is made. And once the family is settled in
its new community, family members go "church shopping." Sometimes they will ask, "Where do we fit best?" But
seldom do they mean, "Why has God sent us to this
community? Where do our spiritual gifts fit? How can
these gifts be used to build up a local fellowship of
believers?" Nor does the local church, which is ap-

proached by Christians seeking to transfer membership, generally concern itself with those questions. "All are welcome" usually means that whoever professes Christ can join. Perhaps an office or position may even be offered to the newcomer, although he or she may first have to successfully complete some probationary service in a "lesser" role. The organic body has been replaced by the bionic man.

I think my friend John Perkins, who, since 1967, has been attempting to work out at Mendenhall, Mississippi, what it means to be a Christian in community, says it well when he tells of a seminarian who was visiting their multi-racial church. After attending the church for a year or so, the seminarian indicated he was still trying to find the church to which he belonged and wondered where it would be. John responded, "If you don't know where you belong, don't come here and mess up this fellowship! God *calls* people into His church."[3]

How many of us really believe that? Again, the values of the culture have become the values of the church.

TURN IT UPSIDE DOWN

Imagine what might happen if we all understood that our primary commitment was to a local body of believers. "Getting ahead" could only be interpreted in terms of how the local church could be strengthened by what we do, or in terms of doing what the local church believes God has called us to do—perhaps in the local fellowship, in another local fellowship, or in some set-apart service for Him. What an announcement that would be to the world. If one-quarter of the working men and women in the United States are truly citizens of God's kingdom, imagine what would happen if, when the companies for which they work ask them to move or to take another job, they were to respond, "I'll let you know after I've talked to my brothers and sisters at St. John's Church." Talk about getting someone's attention!

Such a response would strike at the very heart of

American individualism by announcing that what I do and what I am is intimately related to the body, the community, of which I am a part. It would announce that Christ has my allegiance and that my allegiance is worked out in very practical terms in the day-to-day business of living.

Many years ago Marge and I joined a middle-sized church on the East Coast. We both look back on that experience with a great many positive and warm memories. The people took us in, loved us in, to their fellowship. I served as Sunday school superintendent. Marge led the Daily Vacation Bible School. We recruited people door-to-door to attend the Billy Graham Crusade in nearby New York City. The pastor and his wife were our very close friends among a small circle of very good friends. (We didn't know the phrase "support group" in those days.) When I went through the process of deciding whether or not I should change jobs and move to the Midwest, our pastor said, 'Ed, we *need* you here. We won't be the same without you." I was complimented by his love and concern, but it didn't change my decision to move. As I look back on that move, he was right. They did need me. I was a vital link in that organism, and when I wrenched myself out, it hurt. It continued to hurt that church for years to come.

Praise God He works good out of wrong, but that's not the point. The point is, I never asked my local fellowship what God was saying to them.

Christian commitment starts as an individual thing. *One* becomes committed to Christ. But that commitment is transformed to a commitment to the living body of Christ, a commitment to brothers and sisters who are fellow heirs to the kingdom.

There have been times in history when community commitment as a primary value was also the value of the world in which the church found itself. The same is true in some cultures of the world today; many see the community as the "self." Not so in America.

If American Christianity is to respond effectively to a

culture so turned inward that it finds nothing but despair, then the church, each local fellowship, must demonstrate its commitment to Christ by its commitment to the local group of believers.

NOTES

[1]See Edward R. Dayton and Ted W. Engstrom, *Strategy for Living: How to Make the Best Use of Your Time and Abilities* (Glendale: Regal, 1976) and *Strategy for Leadership* (Old Tappan: Revell, 1978).

[2]See Elizabeth O'Connor, *Journey Inward, Journey Outward* (New York: Harper and Row, 1975).

[3]See John Perkins, *Let Justice Roll Down* (Glendale: Regal, 1976) for a look at a world many white, middle-class Christians know nothing about and to see the power of commitments to overcome this world.

CHAPTER 11

Commitment to the Community

Individualism *is a novel expression, to which a novel idea has given birth. Our fathers were only acquainted with* egoisme *(selfishness). Selfishness is a passionate and exaggerated love of self, which leads a man to connect everything in the world. Individualism is a mature and calm feeling, which disposes each member of the community to sever himself from the mass of his fellows, and to draw apart with his family and his friends; so that, after he has thus formed a little circle of his own, he willingly leaves society at large to itself.*

De Tocqueville

The society that continues to atomize into smaller and smaller groups until each group is a group of one, must eventually collapse. For the glue that holds us together is a series of laws and norms to which a major portion of our society gives assent. When "each man does what is right in his own eyes," anarchy and disintegration are the only possible results.

Intuitively we know this. While demanding freedom, we fear it, because we sense that each one of us is inadequate to face life both in the present and in the eternal. When society no longer provides a general sense of direction or unity we are forced to create our own "society," our own culture, by grouping together with those of reasonably like mind. We will attempt to make a commitment to a community of our own making.

We can see this in much of American society. Americans have been inveterate "joiners" throughout much of our history. Today most Americans seek out associations into and out of which they can easily move. The health club is a good place to find "fellowship" and exercise. The Rotary Club or Kiwanis Club may give us a sense of participating with people of like mind and in something larger than ourselves. The local church may be a convenient way station to have our "batteries charged" for the battle that lies ahead next week. But none of these meet the need we have to be truly part of one another.

But the thought of a deeper commitment, one that announces "I am part of you and you are part of me," is at the same time both an exciting prospect and a frightening one. What would such a commitment mean? How would it be worked out? What are the rules, the norms? We easily conjure up visions of puritanical legalism or the dictatorship of a charismatic leader.

It is my contention that American Christianity is missing a vital ingredient of the Christian life. I believe that a great deal of the powerlessness we experience as individual Christians and as local churches can be attributed to our failure to understand that the beginning point of the Christian life is found in an organic relationship to a local fellowship. The Bible assumes it. An adequate Christian life demands it.

This is not to argue that our failure to become a living part of the body of Christ is peculiar to our times or to our day. Rather it is to point out that for American Christians in this day, in this time, living a completed Christian life in such a fellowship is the most effective way we can stand against a counter-biblical culture and, indeed, help to transform that culture.

The primary American value is individualism: a view of the world that sees everything in relationship to the individual and a view of the individual that sees each of us as completely distinct from all humanity. A natural by-product of this value is materialism, the assumption that life is made more satisfactory by what I can see and touch, what I own, what I as an individual can control, and what I can say is mine.

The primary biblical value is relationship: the relationship between the Creator and the creature; the relationship between God's children; and the relationship between the church and the world.

But Americans have few models of such relationships, and our history gives us no analogies on which to base them. Only in the Christian church do we find any widespread demonstration that such relationships are possible. Only in God's Word do we find the understanding of how such relationships can work. For if we attempt relationships from the American concept of the individual, we always measure the results in terms of what is good for the individual rather than on whether or not others are enhanced. We will always be attempting to do God's will with one hand tied behind our back.

WHERE DO WE BEGIN?

It is apparent that the vast majority of American Christians are not related together in local fellowships in the way the Bible describes. On the other hand, it is equally apparent that millions of Americans are members of organizations that are called local churches. Where do we begin? Is it possible to transform such churches from organizations that have memberships to organisms that have members? Is it possible to call the millions of Lone Ranger Christians into the local fellowships that God has prepared for them and for which he has prepared and gifted them?

I believe the answer to both parts of the question is yes. But I must be quick to admit that much in me has no desire to explore the possibilities. I sense the risk involved. I would prefer to say with Simon and Garfunkel, "I am a rock. I am an island." It takes little intelligence to know that there is a cost to commitment. One has only to read Dietrich Bonhoeffer to gain some small insight into how costly it can be. In some of Bonhoeffer's recently published writing he expressed his fear of returning to Nazi Germany. He considered himself no hero. But a brother there needed him, and the compulsion of the Spirit was so strong that Bonhoeffer *had* to go. In prison and in death he saw himself not as a hero, but as a man who had a commitment to be a disciple of Jesus.

But another side of me cries, "It's worth it all!" The Spirit witnesses to my spirit that sharing in the sufferings of Christ is not a morbid thing. But I need you to be there with me. I need to know that God has spoken to others in like manner.

So the advantage of losing the loneliness of being *me* is well worth the cost of becoming part of a *living* organism.

Let's explore what is involved. What does it means to be committed to an organic part of the body of Christ?

We must first ask what can be said about the *fundamental nature* of any local fellowship. Are there basic characteristics that should be common to all local churches? If so, what are they? Will they help us move toward a new understanding and a new experience of what it means to experience community that is Christian? In the previous chapter we reviewed the process by which people become Christians. We maintained that to be a new creature in Christ is to die to our individual*ism* (not to our individuality); to become a new creature in Christ is to be joined, uniquely and inseparably, to others, with whom we add up to something greater than the sum of the parts. What is lacking in me will be supplied by you. What we both need will be supplied by another exercising his or her gifts. When one falls down, others will lift her up. When one weeps, others will weep with him. Such a relationship is not an organization, although it may be organized; but it is an organism, because it is the combination of living things.[1]

CHARACTERISTICS OF THE CHRISTIAN COMMUNITY

In many ways, discussing the characteristics of a local fellowship is redundant. Hundreds of books have been written on the subject. Many authors, far more qualified than I, have addressed the subject. But if we accept the thesis that the best way to counter our culture is through a deeper commitment to the local church, it is necessary to describe, however briefly, some of the characteristics of such a church. What follows is an attempt to describe basics, fundamentals. We will look at what a local fellowship *is*, review the characteristics of the members of such a body, then discuss what a local fellowship *does*.

Unique

This may seem like a strange place to begin, but it is important to affirm the uniqueness of each local fellowship. If each individual is a unique creation, then the combination of a number of unique people will be a unique organism. Some may want to argue that God can make all fellowships alike if He so desires, but the entire sense of the New Testament from Acts to Revelation is one of allowing different fellowships to maintain their uniqueness. The primary argument for such a view is, of course, the Council of Jerusalem in Acts 15, where the original church at Jerusalem concluded that believers did not have to be circumcised or become Jews in order to be Christians. But notice the flavor of the different fellowships. Even after James' letter to the church in Antioch admonishing the church to refrain from eating meat sacrificed to idols, Paul had no trouble telling the Corinthians to follow their own conscience about the matter. (See 1 Corinthians 8.)

This concept of uniqueness is important. Inherent in our technological culture is the assumption that there is one best way of doing something. Once a formula (or method) is discovered, everyone should use it. But evidence from all over the world demonstrates tremendous varieties within the church. Most Americans would be startled if an independent church from the East African Revival, a Chinese house church from Singapore, a Pentecostal church from Brazil, and a charismatic Catholic fellowship from France were all placed on opposite corners of the same intersection. The comparisons and contrasts would be mind-blowing—not only in the type of services they would have, but in their fundamental beliefs about what constitutes acceptable behavior in the world in which they live. (*They* would have some trouble too!)

Let's take pleasure in the multiplicity of God's creation. Let's free ourselves from putting others down because they are not like us. If we begin here, we won't have to search for the perfect model of the correct organization or the proper ecclesiastical structure. Rather, we can give ourselves over—commit ourselves—to one another and to the Spirit of God and allow Him to move among us and in us as He will. (On the contrary, let's not assume every church *must* be different. When some are very much alike, praise the Lord too!)

Local

I am not opposed to denominations as such. People who are likeminded should be able to share their likemindedness. If there are local churches that believe their understanding of faith and order is similar or identical to that of other local churches, it seems quite appropriate for them to band together, even if separated by distance. And the fact that the Bible never discusses such denominations does not necessarily mean they are wrong. But it is important for us to realize that although there often arose a party-spirit among the churches of the New Testament on such issues as whether or not one had to become a Jew, the Bible basically describes the church in only two parts. First, there is the church universal of which all Christians are a part. Second, there is the church in a particular locality, a particular city. From the account in Acts 6 of the problems that arose regarding the widows of different sections of the church in Jerusalem, we can surmise that there were a number of local worshiping bodies.

We get the same feeling about the churches to whom Paul wrote. In his letter to the church at Rome, Paul greeted Priscilla and Aquila and the church that met in their house (Rom. 16:3–5). In writing to the Corinthians, Paul again refers to Aquila and Priscilla and the church that was meeting in their house, which was evidently somewhere in the province of Asia (1 Cor. 16:19). When Paul writes to the Colossians, he gives greetings to "Nympha and the church in her house" (Col. 4:15). When writing to Philemon, who also lived at Colossi, Paul also writes to "Archippus our fellow soldier and to the church that meets in your home" (Philem. 2).

Localness and uniqueness go hand in hand. Both permit us to appreciate God's ability and desire to work out His good will for us *here*, in this place, and in a way that utilizes all the gifts He has bestowed on us. Both permit us to be committed to a special group of people in a particular place.

In describing "home," the poet Robert Frost said it "is the place where, when you have to go there, they have to take you in." Home is where I expect to find a group of people who will recognize me as a part of them.

The notion of localness should not rob us of the joy of being part of the church universal. It has been my experience and privilege to visit most of the major countries of the world. Even though meeting new people, especially of a different culture, can cause uneasiness, I looked forward with confidence and anticipation to each encounter because I knew that these were brothers and sisters in Christ who would care for me because they loved Jesus. That is something very special.

Intimate

Christians today often wonder what Paul would say about the large churches prevalent in America? I suspect that just as he wrote to the church at Corinth, so he would write to the "Church at 10th Avenue," even if that church had three thousand members. The Bible gives us few clues as to what is the ideal size for a local fellowship. We do, however, have some words about minimum size: "Where two or three come together in my name, there am I with them" (Matt. 18:20). Jewish law said that at least ten males were needed to found a synagogue. But from Paul's and Silas' experience with Lydia in Philippi (Acts 6), we can conclude that it didn't take that many to start a church where there was no synagogue.

What then is a reasonable size for a local church? There is no Biblical answer, but a good case can be made for the notion that a local fellowship should be small enough so that it is possible for every member to know and be known by all the other members. Such a number may vary from culture to culture and with different groups of people, but it is hard to imagine that such a group could exceed a couple hundred. The fact that the vast majority of American churches are smaller may speak to the point.

Many arguments have been put forth as to why large churches are "more effective" and why people prefer to join them, but most of these arguments are culturally conditioned. They consider service to the *individual* and to the community as the primary role of the church and ignore the question of how the body builds itself. Arguments are also made that large churches tend to attract people. But the fact that all local churches in America appear to eventually stop growing makes this argument rather specious.[2]

Peter Wagner has proposed the concept that the large church is actually a *celebration*, within which there are a number of *congregations*. He looks on the small groups within such congregations as *cells*.[3] Wagner is on the right track. If we equate "congregations" with the "local fellowships" discussed above, then each of these congregations should have individuals with the gifts needed to make it a complete expression of the body of Christ, including the gifts of pastor, teacher, administrator.

But larger churches don't usually see themselves as *gifted* congregations. Historically, as a church starts to grow, the members and/or the pastor sense that there is more pastoral work to be done than one person can handle. At this point a pivotal decision is made. Almost always the decision is made to "help the pastor" by providing an assistant. As soon as such a position is created, responsibility for the congregation passes from the people to the "pastoral staff." As a result, the gifts of many of the church members are left unused, undeveloped, and perhaps even unrecognized.

Let's look at another model, another response to the problem of "too many members for the pastor to care for."

Suppose the congregation decided to create another congregation with its own pastor, a congregation that could use the same facilities and build on the experience of the first congregation? The number of people worshiping in a given building might grow rapidly, but the church members would still be capable of being a part of one another.

One church I know has a membership of approximately thirty-five hundred. It holds three Sunday worship services in a sanctuary that holds eleven hundred people. It has ten people who have the title "pastor" attached to their name, but each one has a specialized function. There is an executive pastor, a visitation pastor, a college pastor, a music pastor, etc. If those ten pastors would each head up his own congregation, there would be ten congregations of three hundred, all of which could meet at those three different celebrations on Sunday morning.

Large churches tend to promote individualism and often encourage people to remain anonymous. Large churches that are organized according to the specialized ministries of their pastors have great difficulty meeting the everyday needs of their members. It is possible to have a large church ("celebration") within which there are small congregations, but if a church organizes itself along *functional* lines rather than organic groupings, it will find it impossible to have the type of "body life" that the Bible encourages.

But, some argue, haven't there been large churches throughout history? Where did they come from and how did they work in the past? Historically large churches developed for two reasons. First, they were an attempt to bring glory to God by erecting prominent buildings. The medieval cathedrals, which required year after year of patient and loving construction, were an expression of love for God. They demonstrated both God's presence and the faithfulness of His people. But they did not replace the local parish or the local parish priest or pastor. Second, churches grew because of the growth in population. As more and more people moved into cities, and as transportation facilities improved, the number of people who could gather in any one spot rose sharply. Most large American churches would disappear overnight if rapid and inexpensive means of transportation were not available. (And that day may be closer than we think).

How large should a church be? If we understand the word *church* to mean the group of people who attend service in a particular locality, then small or large makes no difference. But if we understand church to mean *congregation* or *fellowship* then size must somehow be limited.

To put it another way, the size of the church building is the only limiting factor in how many belivers can *attend services* together. But our finite abilities to know and be known by others limit the number of believers with whom we can truly have fellowship, with whom we can truly feel "fit together." There is a limit to our ability to be committed to others. Jesus had his three, the twelve, and the seventy. The issue here is not the need to eliminate large churches, but to define who is part of which congregation and why.

Called Out

The word translated *church* in our New Testament is derived from a word meaning *called out,* as to a meeting or an assembly that has been announced for people to attend. We are people who have been called from one place to another. I agree with John Perkins. Each one of us should be convinced that God has called us to a special congregation in a special place at a particular time. For those accustomed to church-shopping, this is not an easy idea to accept. But for those who have just come to know the Lord and are in the flush of a fantastic new affection, it makes all kinds of sense. To call someone out of the world is to call them to be *in Christ* (one of Paul's favorite expressions). To be in Christ means to be in His body both figuratively and factually. Part of both the obedience and the suffering of the Christian life is commitment to a specific group of people. It's easy to be committed to the whole world; it's more difficult to be committed to our country; it's extremely difficult to be committed to the six families that live on our block. A fundamental characteristic of a biblical local fellowship is that members will know they are where God wants them. Not in a church down the block. Not in a church in another community. But here. Here until He says, "Move."

Fitted Together

If there is any group of people in the world who should understand the expression "fitted together" it should be Americans. How many Christmas Eves have you spent trying to fit together your children's Christmas surprises? How often have you posed over the "easy-to-assemble" directions of the latest gadget you bought for the garden or house? Fitted together means that each part is rightly located to the one next to it. The designer made a slot that was intended for a certain size tab or a hole that was supposed to accept a given size screw. We don't put the spark plugs of the car engine under the dashboard.

In order to fit things together we need to understand their particular characteristics. So it is with the body of Christ. These special characteristics are called "spiritual gifts." They are designed for the common good. Without each one the assembly is not complete, not finished. *Every* part is needed.

During my army induction process I took a mechanical aptitude test. Given a drawing of an automobile generator and an actual assembled generator, we were instructed to take it apart, show it to the instructor, and then reassemble it. Mine just wouldn't go back together. Finally the instructor pointed to the drawing and showed me that the metal washer I had been trying to put on the inside belonged on the outside of the shaft. That's how it is with the local assembly. One part in the wrong place can really foul things up.

Gifted

In a local fellowship, the spiritual gifts of individual members determine the form and shape the congregation will take. This important idea goes hand in hand with the idea of uniqueness. God evidently chooses to create fellowships with a different mix of gifts. Some fellowships may have an abundance of members with the gift of evangelism. The result will be a church that is constantly calling people to Christ. Other fellowships may discover they have many members with gifts of mercy. Their ministry may be one of mercy within their community. Others may discover an unusual number of members with the missionary gift. They may become a church that sends missionaries into various parts of the world.

Notice that Christians *come equipped* with these gifts. Yes, we can desire other gifts, and we can pray for some. But the Bible teaches that at the moment we come to Christ we are ready to be fitted into a body that in some mysterious way *needs us* immediately. And, since God gives gifts to enable believers to function within a larger body of believers, it follows that the body itself is able to identify the gifts of its members and also has a way to discover the gifts of those members yet to be incorporated into it.

We need to note at this point that certain gifts must be present in every local church. For instance, each fellowship needs at least one person with the gift of pastor and at least one with the gift of teacher. (As a manager, I'd like to see someone in every church with the gift of administration too!)

Spirit-marked

A Christian fellowship is made up of individuals who have renounced their commitment to the world and have made a commitment to Christ. Why "Spirit-marked"? The one characteristic that differentiates Christians, citizens of the kingdom, from the rest of humanity is the indwelling of the Holy Spirit. He is our guarantee that we belong to God. "If anyone does not have the Spirit of Christ, he does not belong to Christ" (Rom. 8:9). "Those who are led by the Spirit of God are sons of God" (Rom. 8:14). This fellowship is therefore made up of those who have been marked by the Spirit, who are led by the Spirit, and who are gifted by the Spirit.[4] This is not to say that all who attend meetings of such a fellowship must already have accepted Christ. But the primary focus of the regular meeting times of a local fellowship should not be to attract non-Christians to the Savior. The task of the fellowship is to build itself up so that it can go forth.

A Family Affair

This fellowship is meant for children, teenagers, and adults. It emphasizes the value of the family. It understands that the family is the basic unit of society and does whatever it can to strengthen relationships within that family. In developing commitments at the second level of relationships (between God's children), family relationships and commitments (between husband, wife, and children) should be at the top of our priority list.

THE CHARACTERISTICS OF CHRISTIANS

Before discussing what every local fellowship *does* as a body, it is useful to remind ourselves of the qualities of the individuals who make up this organism. These qualities have nothing to do with gifts as such. It is true that some will carry out their relationships toward one another with special enthusiasm or special ability, but everyone in this body, without exception, is commanded to do certain things. The outline that follows was produced by my friend Dale Kretzman, and was part of his input for a class we teach together.

> *Christians are to love one another.*
> *(John 13:34; 15:12; 1 Peter 4:8)*

To love one another means we have faith in each other (Rom. 1:12). The opposite side of this is that we are not to attack one another (Gal. 5:15), nor are we to judge one another (Rom. 14:13).

> *Christians are to forgive one another.*
> *(Eph. 4:32)*

We will continue to sin. We will probably sin against one another. But forgiveness is the important factor. We are to see one another as being on a journey. As Paul told the Philippians, we have not arrived. We are moving toward Christ. We are moving into Christ.

Personally, I don't have much trouble forgiving those who come to me and ask forgiveness. Indeed, I am often surprised. A few months ago a man I worked with ten years earlier came to ask my forgiveness for the feelings he had about me when we worked together. That kind of forgiveness I find easy to give.

But I have trouble forgiving those who *keep* sinning against me. I want to place limits on my forgiveness. Seventy times seven seems a little much! The Bible, however, places no limits on forgiveness; it is to be complete.

Christians are to care for one another.
(I Peter 4:10, John 13:14)

When we are hurt and battered we are to *comfort* one another (1 Thess. 4:18). We are always to be thinking about how well the other is doing (Phil. 2:4). What a contrast this is to "looking out for Number One"!

Pilgrims band together for their own mutual good. There is much heartache along the road that leads to the Celestial City.

For many years Marge and I were deeply involved with a Sunday school class of young married couples. One day a young child of one of the couples was in serious condition in the local hospital. So many members of that class wanted to be there caring and praying that the hospital staff finally had to make special arrangements to handle them all.

Christians are to teach one another.
(Gal. 5:13)

Some members obviously are gifted as teachers. But each of us has something to teach others, for each of us has special qualities others don't have.

Americans are not very teachable. I enjoy teaching, but I don't always enjoy being taught, especially if the brother or sister teaching is not as "experienced" as I. But I have come to learn that there are very few Christians who cannot contribute to my life, *if I will let them.* (My friend Ted Engstrom said to me once years ago, "The trouble with you, Ed, is that you won't *let* people love you!")

Christians are to be subject to one another.
(1 Peter 5:5; Eph. 5:21)

Being subject to one another is another way of saying we are to prefer one another (Rom. 12:10). A great deal has been written about the business of being subject to one another, particularly in the relationship between husbands and wives. The key is obviously the phrase *to one another*.

My same friend, Ted, has taught me a lot about this. Ted is a Christian statesman, the president of the largest evangelical Christian service agency in the world. He has been my boss and colleague for seventeen years. We are members of the same church. He's the boss as far as the world is concerned, but within our brotherhood as Christians and our place in the body, we are subject to one another. Sometimes he leads; sometimes I do.

Christians are to be together.

We are to have fellowship with each other (1 John 1:7), to greet one another (Rom. 16:16; 1 Cor. 16:20), to speak to each other (Eph. 5:19), and to receive or accept each other (Rom. 15:7).

Christians are to be hospitable.
(1 Peter 4:9)

Some Christians have the gift of hospitality. It is a delight to be in their homes. But one of the marks of any Christian home is that others are always welcome. The living room may be askew. The beds may be unmade. There may be very little to serve for supper. But none of these things matter when we sense we are genuinely welcome.

Peter Wagner, who has written a lot about spiritual gifts, is also a member of my church. Pete claims that he and his wife, Doris, don't have the gift of hospitality. Perhaps they don't. But I know they practice it!

Christians are to honor one another.
(Rom. 12:10)

The emphasis in American culture on comparing one thing with another and on judging one thing against another makes it very easy for us to focus on negatives. Recently I read an article that suggested it is time we "caught our children doing something good, for a change."

John Rymer, dean of the Cathedral of the Holy Trinity in

Auckland, New Zealand, has another way of putting it. He says we are tempted often to do good, but fail to give in to temptation! The rich young ruler and the priest who walked to the other side of the street to avoid being bothered by a wounded man were a lot like today's Americans.

Christians are to be concerned for one another.

In the case of sin, we are to *rebuke* one another (Luke 17:3). When correction is needed, we are to *admonish* one another (Rom. 15:4; Col. 3:16). And when encouragement is needed, we are to *exhort* one another (Heb. 3:13).

Christians are to confess to one another. ### *(James 5:16)*

Confession is extremely difficult. It's hard enough to admit our sin to God, but to admit it to one another—that hurts. But confession is the only way to deal with guilt. The psychiatrist Hobart Mowrer observes that early Christianity wonderfully provided for the expiation of guilt by confessing sin to one another. The Roman church then bent this somewhat by saying that it was necessary only to confess to the priest. The Protestants made it worse by saying that one didn't have to confess to the priest, only to God. Finally, Freud came along and said there was really no sin to confess. We need to get back past Freud, past our Protestant individualism, past confession to the priest, and regain the biblical ability to cleanse ourselves by confessing to one another.[5] How this is to be done will vary from congregation to congregation.

Some years ago I had reservations to fly from New York to Los Angeles, but my flight was overbooked. To compensate for the inconvenience, the airline gave each unaccommodated passenger a check for two hundred dollars and put the would-be passengers on the next flight. "What a break," I thought, already spending the money mentally. But the money really wasn't mine. I was on business for World Vision. The next day during our morning sharing time at the office someone commented about my missed flight and asked about the rebate situation. Before I knew what had happened, I indicated there was none. I lived with that lie for about ten minutes and then called the staff into my office and confessed I had lied. My, that hurt. But how good it felt to be forgiven.

What do Christians do? They *act toward one another*. Everything we have discussed has to do with relationships one to another. Can there be any doubt that if outsiders were to find a fellowship with these attributes they would be so overcome with joy that they would say, "This is the kind of group I would like to be a part of. Where do I sign up?"

Notice that none of these attributes is dependent on how we organize our churches. Nor does it matter whether we are rich or poor. None of these behaviors is peculiar to any one culture or society. Each may work itself out differently, but each is universal to all peoples everywhere.

WHAT DOES EVERY LOCAL FELLOWSHIP DO?

When we rapidly rehearsed the four hundred years of history that formed the American culture of our day, we noted that our country was founded by those who had a profound sense of the kingdom of God, by those who not only announced that it had arrived but who attempted to live as they understood citizens of God's kingdom should live. So should we. It is not enough to proclaim God's kingdom. We must also demonstrate it. The title of Don Kraybill's book says it well: we are talking about *The Upside-down Kingdom*. The kingdom we announce, the kingdom we attempt to live, is upside-down from the world's view of things. That is why it is so difficult for us to live a kingdom life as *individuals*. Have you ever been in a foreign land where there were no other Americans? When all alone, it is difficult to live like an American. But bring along twenty or thirty friends and it is a different story. So it is with Christians.

What is it like to live a kingdom life in a community? What does such a community *do*? What follows is not an exhaustive list. Rather it is designed to focus on several primary characteristics.

A *community builds itself up.*

Building itself up, though it sounds self-centered, is one of the most important functions of every local fellowship. Why? So that it can efficiently perform kingdom business. Americans know a great deal about team training. We know that even though there are stars on an athletic team, it takes an entire team, all in good shape, to consistently play a good game. And, conversely, one of the results of building the team is that individuals are automatically built. "When the team wins, everybody wins." "Do not conform any longer to the pattern of this world, but be transformed by the renewing of your mind. Then you will be able to test and approve what God's will is—his good, pleasing and perfect will" (Rom. 12:2). Or, as J. B. Phillips translates this same passage, "Don't let the world press you into its mould."

A *community is willing to die.*

By willing to die I do not mean members must be willing to sacrifice themselves as individuals. That's important, but what I mean here is that the community is willing to go out of existence if that is God's desire for it. We have grown so used to the idea that the church on the corner is a permanent fixture that the thought of it closing its doors seems almost antibiblical. We confuse the church *building* with the church. Conceivably, a local fellowship may be needed for only a few years. It may meet a special need the Lord has at that time.

To put it another way, the "success" of the local fellowship is not evidenced by longevity. Its commitment is to be obedient, not to survive. Nowhere in the Bible does it say that a local fellowship is supposed to last five years, ten years, or a hundred years. One could, in fact, probably make a pretty good case for assuming that most local churches should undergo a major re-formation every generation.

A community seeks to identify gifts.

The community assumes that each of its members is gifted for the good of the whole. It attempts to discover and encourage the use of those gifts. It assumes that God sends into its midst one who is specially prepared. It especially identifies those who have the gift of pastor.[6]

A community gathers together for worship.

It is important to note the difference between worship and education. What evangelicals often call worship services are actually times of teaching. There is nothing wrong with teaching, but teaching and worship are two different things. When we worship, God is the audience; we are the performers. What we do and how we do it is based on our understanding of what we are called to do. Form may vary. Singing may be lusty or staid. We may stretch forth our hands in adoration or use kneeling pillows. We may just sit in silence, praising God with our inner being. No matter. No matter, as long as we know to whom we are directing our worship.

Communion, the eucharist, is a regular part of worship, for in it we respond to Christ's command to remember Him and His sacrifice through this simple yet mystical act.

A community gathers together for fellowship.

Again, the form of fellowship is not as important as the intent. The intent of fellowship is to know and be known, to listen and be listened to, to share in others' joys and sorrows and have them share in ours. It is a fellowship of families, as well as individuals. It models for its children how Christian love is worked out.

A community seeks to be taught.

God's Word and God's Spirit are the church's source of truth, but the resources available for teaching are legion. One thing that does need to be said is that the church accepts the whole counsel of God. That is, it is willing to live in the paradox of the sovereignty of God and the free will of people, the paradox of God's revealed and written Word and God's continuing revelation, the paradox of a kingdom that has arrived and is yet to come, the paradox that we are cleansed from sin and yet continue to sin.

A community rightly divides the sacred and the profane.

"It is a fearful thing to fall into the hands of the living God!" Would that we experienced this fearfulness in our everyday life. To have a knowledge of what is holy is to be overcome with the awesomeness (awe-full-ness) of God. A biblical local fellowship will attempt to maintain a healthy balance between knowing Jesus as the one who loves me like no one else loves me and knowing Jesus as Lord of the universe. When we lose the sense of the sacred in life, we easily succumb to the technological fix as the answer to life's problems.

But another side of the question of the sacred is the false division we make between what we consider sacred and what we consider secular. We tend to assume, simply on the basis of vocation, that some people are more sacred than others. The local church should know no spiritual pecking order. To be called to "full-time Christian service" is not reserved for the pastor or the missionary. To be sacred, to be holy, is to be conformed to the image of Christ, not to a profession.

A community seeks to understand how it is being coerced by its culture and seeks to respond appropriately.

The local church realizes it is constantly influenced, especially in matters of lifestyle, by its surrounding culture. Although Scripture offers few specific prescriptions for what the Christian lifestyle should be, the local fellowship knows that its lifestyle must be distinctive from the world, and it will continue to examine and refine the lifestyle it has adopted.

A community permits differences in others.

The church does not believe that the truth God has revealed is all the truth that exists. He left some things unsaid. Therefore, just as the church in Jerusalem accepted the differences in the church at Antioch, the local fellowship today accepts the differences of other fellowships and believes each can be in the will of God. As a result, the community sees itself as part of a larger whole and desires to be in fellowship with all who name the name of Christ as Lord.

A community is on a journey, not at its destination.

Much of evangelical Christianity in America assumes a person is either "in" or "out." It even goes about setting up rules and measurements to determine one's "inness" or "outness." As a result, growth is often stunted. We said earlier that Paul never considered himself as having "arrived." So how can *we*? The fundamental question is, "Do we desire to know Christ as Lord and Savior?" We are either moving toward Him or away from Him.

A community is worldly.

The local fellowship does not become part *of* the world but sees itself as being *in* the world. The natural response of the Christian should be one of compassion. We live in a hurting society. We live and move in the same smog, the same political corruption, and the same mechanistic economic system as do men and women who do not yet know Christ. We need to be against the world but for the world. One of the dimensions that is still missing in what some have called the Third Evangelical Awakening is the dimension of social concern. And as we talk about the world, we need to be careful not to generalize to the point of impossibility. Bob Pierce used to say, "Just because we can't do everything, doesn't mean we shouldn't do something." We can't be responsible for the entire world, but we need to decide what part we *will* be responsible for.

A community believes it is building God's kingdom.

The local church is part of God's instrument to establish His kingdom. God is at work in all of history. God's rain falls on the just and the unjust. His plans are for all of creation.

A community sets some apart.

The local church is called to build itself up. But it is also to respond to the moving of the Holy Spirit who says, "Set apart for me Barnabas and Saul for the work to which I have called them" (Acts 13:2). Set-apart people are healthy people in the sense that they can make it on their own apart from the nurture of the local community. They are people who, in the apostolic tradition, move out to communicate between churches and to proclaim Christ where He is not known. But again we need to resist individualism. The Holy Spirit should speak to the church as well as to the individual. I sometimes challenge local churches to pray for an entire year as to whom God would have them set apart for a non-parochial ministry, be it cross-cultural missions or service in America. What a difference this would make in the way we think about "sending missionaries!" Instead of their coming hat in hand to us, looking for "support," we would challenge *them* and *send* them forth!

A community understands the cost of discipleship.

The world says, "Hey, don't get too involved with people. You can get *hurt!*" The Christian fellowship replies, "Yes, we know. Christ told us all about that." In the words of Dietrich Bonhoeffer, "The response of disciples is an act of obedience, not a confession of faith in Jesus." [7]

In many ways discipleship would be easier if it were a once-and-for-all commitment to give up my "rights" to the Lord through the medium of the community. But life does not come nicely packaged with a time slot for this and a time slot for that. As I sit here and write I have given myself over to a task that demands my time and a great deal of energy. But at any moment the phone may ring and the need expressed at the other end of the line will have to take precedence over this book. People don't seem to have marriage problems according to a plan. They lose their jobs, contract cancer, and come down with the latest virus pretty much at random. Giving up my rights turns out to mean fitting myself to meet your need. It costs.

WHAT ARE THE DIFFERENCES?

So far in this book I have not mentioned organizational structure, methods of ministry, lifestyle, or a host of other things that are covered by a plethora of how-to-do-it books. Those things are important; but they are important only after we make an initial commitment to the idea that community is indeed the biblical norm to which we are called.

WHAT IS COMMUNITY?

In all of the above we have talked about what a local fellowship is, according to the New Testament, and what it does. Notice that none of these things are culturally conditioned. Relationships seldom are. True, different cultures have different ways of expressing love, kindness, patience, longsuffering, mercy, and goodness. But each *knows* instinctively when those things are present. They do not result from a particular organizational structure.

People who understand these kinds of relationships and who are attempting to work them out can only be described as people who are *in community*. And they *know* it. If we asked members of such a group about their relationships with others, they would immediately tell us about the community of which they are an organic part. But the way they were *organized* might surprise us. What you or I might consider to be the characteristics of a "community" might be quite different from their view.

UNTYING THE HAND BEHIND THE BACK

Attempting to live a Christian life while trying to maintain our strong American individualism is like trying to do a job that requires two hands while having one hand tied behind our back. But we can't just say, "I renounce my individualism!" That is like cleansing a house of demons only to have other demons enter. We can't suddenly renounce a basic part of our culture without an immense amount of both conscious and unconscious pressure from our fellow citizens. What we need is an effective substitute. Society, including our Christian friends, needs some way of understanding what we are doing.

When Marge and I were forty, God called us in a very definite way to leave the aerospace industry and go to seminary to study for further ministry. When we left Grand Rapids, we left behind a large colonial home with five bedrooms and a bathroom for each of us. When we arrived in Pasadena to go to Fuller Seminary, we moved into a small house with two bedrooms and one small bath. We put our three teenage girls in one bedroom (to sleep in a *triple* bunk). A year later we had another child.

During those three years I attended seminary our small home was quite acceptable to us and to the new Christian friends we made. We all assumed that when I took a pastorate, we would move into something that would permit somewhat more gracious entertaining than was possible in our eight-by-nine dining room. But the Lord had other plans. I joined World Vision to begin a new ministry of world evangelism, and we stayed in that little house for thirteen years.

Whether it was our perception, the perception of our friends, or a combination of both, I am not sure, but some of our friends no longer seemed comfortable in our small house, even though Marge had it beautifully decorated with the family antiques. Our living in that small home while our middle-class friends lived in much more commodious accommodations was a problem for them (and, I am afraid, for us). It wasn't *acceptable*. Our lifestyle was *different* from theirs. It was all right when we were going to seminary and had very little money, but now that I had a full-time job and could (theoretically!) afford more, it was no longer all right. In other words, our culture was setting the agenda for how we and our friends perceived our living situation.

The strongest antidote for the part of our American culture that is counter-Christian is to live as part of one another, as part of Christ's body, as part of a local fellowship that accepts what and who it is and attempts to discover how God would have it work out His will. The way to untie that arm from behind our back is to ask other Christians to do it for us.

NOTES

[1]See Lawrence O. Richards and Clyde Hoeldtke, *A Theology of Church Leadership* (Grand Rapids: Zondervan, 1980), for a stimulating discussion on the church as an organism and the difference between organism and organization in the church.

[2]Entirely different models are found in Latin America. Brasil para Cristo is a "church" with over 100,000 members. The mother church seats 25,000, but the members meet weekly in their local fellowships.

[3]See Peter Wagner, "Celebration-Congregation-Cell," *Your Spiritual Gifts Can Help Your Church Grow* (Glendale: Regal, 1979).

[4]I will leave the discussion on what it means to be Spirit-*filled* to others. The Old and New Testaments both refer to special times when the Spirit somehow "filled" a person. Others, such as the seven "deacons" in Acts 6, were observed as

being filled with the Spirit. I'm all for it, but I think it remains one of God's special gifts, and a mysterious one at that.

[5]See O. Hobart Mowrer, *The New Group Therapy* (New York: Van Nostrand, 1964).

[6]How strange that in our Western system, *individuals* are "called" to the ministry, go to seminary, and *then* look for a church.

[7]Dietrich Bonhoeffer, *The Cost of Discipleship* (New York: Macmillan, 1967), 16.

CHAPTER 12

The Cost of Community

Thus, not only does democracy make every man forget his ancestors, but it hides his descendants and separates his contemporaries from him; it throws him back forever upon himself alone, and threatens in the end to confine him entirely within the solitude of his own heart.   De Tocqueville

Some years ago Frank Sinatra popularized the song "I Did It My Way." Some years later I heard a popular gospel singer change the words slightly to "I Did It *His* Way." But the emphasis was still on the *I*. Is it possible that we can really be a Christian and not be an everyday part of the body of Christ? Can we be Christians and not be in community?

Many peoples of the world would say that one cannot even be a human being and not be in community. To them, someone who is not in the community is an outcast. Remember the story of the group described in *Reader's Digest* who had had no contact with outsiders? Their sense of community was so great that they had no concept of the individual as a self.

To many of Paul's readers down through the ages, truths such as the ones repeated in this book would not have required unnatural responses. When Paul talked about believers all being one body, the concept was not new to them. In their society that was how they thought of themselves. Thus, we should not be surprised when we hear about "people movements" in which entire groups turn to Christ at one time. In their minds that is the only way they could do it. The same is true for many family groups of the world. Western missionaries have often made the mistake of attempting to lead an individual to Christ when, in the eyes of that person's family, making such a commitment without the entire family is a terrible and unloving thing to do.[1]

Can I be a Christian and not be in community? Most American Christians would like to believe that is possible. We rejoice in our eternal security. We *have* made it!

I must confess an internal struggle here. Evidence in Scripture indicating that we might not really have an unlosable salvation is enough to keep me nervous. When I read about those on Jesus' left in Matthew 25, I shudder. For decades American evangelists have been calling us to repent and be saved. Few have called us to repent and join the *Company of the Committed*. (Let me encourage you to read Elton Trueblood's book by that name. It was written over twenty years ago; but not much has changed.) Some days I am a Calvinist Arminian and other days an Arminian Calvinist, but I always fall back on the promise that the Lord knows who are His and will not let them escape out of His hand.

American Christianity, American evangelical Christianity, has been so enmeshed in American culture that we Christians have trouble telling the difference. To come apart, to become a small company of men and women and children who believe that this community is more important than any individual accomplishment, would be a statement that America could not ignore. If the community turns inward, it will be branded as odd. If it speaks only to the world to condemn the world, it will be called radical (not a bad word for Christians!). If it finds a balance between the two, it will attract Americans from every walk of life.

Daniel Yankelovich heads a research firm that tracks American beliefs and values. In his latest book, *New Rules: Searching for Self-fulfillment in a World Turned Upside Down,* he notes that despite the turmoil of the 60s and 70s, Americans, surprisingly, have not lost their longing for morality. Some feel almost trapped in *having* to do what society demands. When confronted by her counselor about her destructive lifestyle, one woman replied, "Do you mean I don't *have* to act this way?"! Yankelovich concludes his book with a chapter entitled "Toward an Ethic of Commitment." He senses that Americans have had enough of the culture of narcissism and enough of searching inside themselves for answers. It hasn't worked. They are slowly recognizing we are designed to be committed to others. They are ready for such commitments. If they don't find them in Christ, rest assured they will look for them elsewhere.

If we are to cry out to the world, "Save yourselves from this wicked perverse generation," we must first speak to ourselves. It is not easy.

SOME OBVIOUS OBJECTIONS

The kind of commitment we have been discussing is costly. Let me respond to what I believe will be the most common objections to this new way of life.

It's scary. I don't want to lose my identity.

I have to admit that in my heart I really want to be me. It's one thing to "give myself completely to Christ," but to give myself completely to a group of imperfect Christians. . . ? That's frightening.

Yes, it is. But do we believe God, or don't we? If this is what He has planned for us, does He not desire to make us all what we should and can be? God's Word promises He will give us a new life, a better life.

And commitment is not so scary when we are in it

together. Perhaps the first step is for me to admit to you that I am scared too. (That's not very American, either, is it?) For many of us, coming to Christ was scary. But the joy, the freedom, the knowledge that "someone really knows who I am and how I feel" is a very precious thing.

I'm not ready for "the simple lifestyle."

Neither am I. I'm not sure anyone ever is. But the problem with lifestyle is not what we are doing, but our preoccupation with what we *think* other people will think of what we're doing. Peter Drucker, a well-known management authority, came to this country for the first time during the Great Depression. He was intrigued by the way everyone seemed to be pulling for everyone else. Even the immigration officer gave him some advice about finding a better job. Neighbors rejoiced when someone else found work. "We were all in it together," he said.[2]

What Christianity is really all about is creating a Christ-directed culture, one in which there are "people like us," people who live the same way we do. All the how-to-do-it books in the world on the simple lifestyle (and there are many good ones)[3] will give us little help if there aren't others "like us." Lifestyle is more a matter of attitude than of possessions. And who knows what lifestyle the Lord may lead your fellowship to adopt?

Lifestyle is as much an attitude as it is a way of doing things. There is a "Christian lifestyle" for each community. As I have noted before, it will be different for each community because each is called and gifted in different ways. The important thing is that the community ask the question, "Are we living in a way that honors Christ? Are we following the movings of the Spirit in our hearts? Are we doing what the Bible says we should do?"

Some of us will be called to a radically different lifestyle. I praise God for communities that have decided they need to live and work among the poor and downtrodden and hopeless people of urban America. I praise God too for people like Graham Kerr, TV's former Galloping Gourmet, who has committed himself and his community to show us how we can build a new lifestyle one step at a time.[4]

A group such as that can become legalistic. I don't want to live by a bunch of dos and don'ts.

You're right. Any time a group of people thinks it has found the answer, group members start making up ways and means to preserve what they have. We must always search for the balance between legalism and license. The fulcrum is what James calls "liberty."

The tension we face is the typical American dilemma. How can we have both (individual) freedom and equality? The answer is, we can't. The Christian solution is to become a slave to the One in whom there is perfect freedom. And there's that upside-down kingdom again.

But there is a positive side of this. We *need* rules. The reason we teach our children good manners is so that when they are in society they will not be uncomfortable, nor will they make the people around them uncomfortable. Young people need rules. Marge and I have a "second family." Rob came along thirteen years after our youngest daughter. Our experience with three girls didn't prepare us for a boy, particularly one who is gifted and energetic and outspoken and a leader and bigger than I am. But Rob wants to know what his limits are. And so do we in our relationships.

When we work out the "rules" together, they become *our* rules, and that can be a very satisfying thing. It can also be dangerous, however, if we allow ourselves to believe our rules, and only our rules, are right.

I might lose my job or have to change it.

That's right, you might. I have talked to men who were well on their way up the corporate ladder when they decided God wanted them to stay where they were and continue to be a part of a local fellowship. They lost their jobs. But those same men testify to the way God has used that experience not only to make them more mature in

Christ but to give them a new sense of values and a new closeness to their families.[5]

The organization of which I am part has been growing rapidly for the past ten years. We continually need men and women with experience and maturity. Many of the people who respond to our openings come from well-paying positions in industry. They are faced not only with a reduction in salary, but often with the unbelievably high cost of housing in Southern California. Many must move their families into substantially reduced circumstances. One of the things we say to them is, "Don't come to World Vision unless you are convinced there is no other place you could go and be in God's will." Most of them discover, as have Marge and I, that it is not only "worth it all," but that it's better in every way.

I can't be accountable to others.

To the go-go American professional, the thought of having others "control" their lives doesn't sound at all appealing. It runs against the grain of growing desire for individual freedom. But we need to remind ourselves that in dying we begin to live. We died once in order to have a new life in Christ. (We have been saved.) But it is also a process. (We are being saved.) We need to die daily so we can be resurrected daily. It's that upside-down kingdom again. Give yourself away and you will find yourself. Keep tight control and life will ooze out from between your fingers.

There are a lot of strange Christians around, and I don't get along with many of them.

Neither do I. I wish it wasn't so, but I find myself looking for people like me because they affirm that I'm OK. But the Lord has ways of putting us together with people we might never choose as friends. And often, once we get beyond our first impressions, we discover these individuals have much to give us and much to receive from us.

C.S. Lewis, in responding to those who said they knew a

lot of Christians who were no better than people who were pagans, replied, "You should have seen them before Christ took over their lives!" We all have our deformities. Some are quite apparent. Some are deep inside. But those "deformities" are like the missing pieces near the edge of an almost completed jigsaw puzzle. They need to be filled in. The concept of the body is that God shapes other people to fit into our areas of weakness and that together we can become strong. Unity is not just a matter of agreeing. Unity is a group of people who are *acting* together.

A missionary friend tells of trying to demonstrate this concept to a group of women. She designated each one of them as part of the body. Two were feet, others were the torso, one was the head, two were arms, and two others were hands. She then placed a bottle of perfume on the shelf and asked the "body" to open the bottle and anoint itself. After the "body" was able to move itself to the shelf, it discovered how difficult it is for arms and hands that belong to different people to even open the bottle. But that's what unity is all about. It demands that we act together.

What happens if we grow? Won't we lose the closeness we have worked so hard to achieve?

The loss of intimacy is a high price to pay for church growth. Since the number of close relationships we can develop is limited, we would like to settle in with those we have grown to love and appreciate. One thing every church has to decide is whether it is going to grow by division or by incorporation. When a local fellowship reaches a size beyond which it can no longer maintain the characteristics of a biblical fellowship, a church that has decided to grow by division divides into two smaller fellowships that can maintain intimacy but continue to grow. I know of one congregation that decided that as soon as their building was filled, they would hire a "missionary" to start another fellowship and give the new group all the existing facilities.

Growing by incorporation assumes that effective congregations will be maintained even in a larger celebration.

SOME NOT-SO-OBVIOUS OBJECTIONS

Other problems with the kind of fellowship we are advocating, though not as immediately obvious as the objections raised above, still need to be considered.

Inwardness

Once we have found each other, the experience can often be so exciting, so refreshing, that we don't want to disturb it. The thought of bringing "someone new" into our group threatens us. Suppose they don't agree with us? Suppose it doesn't work? The greatest temptation of a community in Christ is to take a journey inward without the accompanying journey outward.[6] The initial temptation, once the nervousness of discovering one another is past, is to want to go deeper into one another's lives, to build a pleasant garden into which the world cannot intrude. In one sense this is a form of monasticism. It deals with the world by separating from it. "More striking is the larger number (of communities) which have ended. One decisive factor in communities' survival is whether they learn to establish deep relationships with other traditions and movements within the church that can nurture and call them past their hidden sins and the imbalances of their creative vision."[7]

Outwardness

The opposite of the journey inward is to come together as a task group for an "outward" ministry (a typical American approach). Here camaraderie is found in accomplishing a task together. There is a world out there that needs help. God has called us to change the world. Let's go! The danger here is that the precarious balance between building up the church and doing the work of the church will be lost. How easy it is to keep our individuality, to contribute our gift not for others but for "the cause."

How do we keep our balance between inwardness and outwardness? Often it is like walking along a six-foot high wall that is only a few inches wide. It's a struggle to keep from falling. How much easier it would be to jump off and be done with the tension. Again we must remind ourselves of the uniqueness of the church. It is the one organization in the world that sets itself two contradictary goals: to care for its members, no matter how weak or hurting they may be; and to send its members forth to sacrifice, perhaps even to sacrifice their lives.

Communication

How will we maintain communication? How will we develop a nervous system for this organism? Should we divide into smaller fellowship groups? Would it be better to pair up or to have group leaders? This is an area about which much has been written, so there are many answers. But the most important thing is to be concerned enough to ask the question. Our problem is not how to do it. Our problem is committing ourselves to begin the task.

Communication is costly. An old African proverb says, "Nothing happens until people talk." We need to be together to talk. But we also have to take into account the kind of people we are. We are not going to become Africans in our thinking. It is unlikely that many of the American cultural values that have been ingrained in us will disappear. Many of them shouldn't. They are good and positive values that can be used for the glory of Christ and His kingdom. We need to use all the channels open to us. In our society it is almost impossible to overcommunicate. Some people will believe something (hear it) only if they see it in writing. Others will hear it only when it is written and spoken by an important person in their life. Still others hear it only when it is said the same way five times.

Communication goes on at many levels. Our church has a weekly mimeographed flyer called "Helping Hand" which provides information about people who need a job, people who need a place to stay, and people who have those things to offer. We have a Sunday bulletin that tells us about what's happening the following week. We have a monthly newspaper to encourage us about what God is doing in our midst. Yet most of us feel we are underinformed.

Ted Engstrom and I have tried to deal with some of this in our book *Strategy for Leadership.* There are many other good resources. Find them.

Organization

A very American response to any situation is "Let's get organized." There have been many models. Some have "worked." Others haven't. I am convinced that there is no one best model, nor are there ten or twelve or a hundred. Each unique group will have to find the Holy Spirit's unique answer for them.

In *Strategy for Leadership* Ted and I pointed out that any effective organization needs several basic elements. First, it needs a *purpose*, a reason for being. Second, it needs clear *goals*, statements about what it expects to be and do in the future. Third, it needs *committed and gifted people.* Fourth, those people need the *resources* to carry out what they have committed themselves to do. Fifth, they need *good communication* among the people. Imagine a group of people who have a common purpose, who know what they want to be and do, who have the gifts and resources to reach their goals. Furthermore, there is good communication between them. Who can believe that such a group will not accomplish what it sets out to do? So the sixth element is the last: organization. Given the first five, the organization necessary to facilitate all the relationships and roles will be easily identified.

Cost

It would be unfair to say that many of us have "bought in" to the American way of life. Most of us have been so immersed in American culture that we didn't realize there was any other way. We are like that frog in the tank of water. The water temperature was comfortable at first; he had no reason to suspect danger. When the temperature began to rise slowly, the change was so gradual he still felt safe, unaware that the rising temperature would one day kill him.

But everything of value has a cost, and we need to recognize that there is a cost to "buying out" of the American way of life. The beautiful thing is, though, that God has prepared for us a place of great value—a place in community, a place where we can make commitments of lasting value. And there is nothing—nothing—in the American way of life, nor in any other way of life, of higher value.

NOTES

[1]For a beautiful story of the impact of individuals who saw themselves as a complete community, one in which individuals could only be baptized into Christ if *all* were baptized, see Vincent J. Donovan, *Christianity Rediscovered*, rev. ed. (Maryknoll: Orbis, 1982).

[2]See Peter Drucker, *Adventures of a Bystander* (New York: Harper and Row, 1979).

[3]See Ronald J. Sider, *Rich Christians in an Age of Hunger: A Biblical Study* (Downers Grove: InterVarsity Press, 1977). I would also argue that the simple lifestyle needs a purpose *outside* the community.

[4]For more information on this exciting experiment, write to Mr. Graham Kerr, Operation L.O.R.D., P.O. Box 13058, Tacoma, WA 98401.

[5]There is a growing resistance in the secular world to changing locality. Whether this is a result of economic or social changes remains to be seen. However, it may well be part of a growing narcissism that insists on "doing it my way" (as opposed to the company's way).

[6]See Elizabeth O'Connor, *Journey Inward, Journey Outward* (New York: Harper and Row, 1975). The Church of the Savior in Washington, D.C., is a community that has struggled with this dilemma.

[7]Bob Sabath, "A Community of Believers," *Sojourners*, January 1980,   17.

CHAPTER 13

Where to Begin

He who descended is the very one who ascended higher than all the heavens, in order to fill the whole universe. It was he who gave some to be apostles, some to be prophets, some to be evangelists, and some to be pastors and teachers, to prepare God's people for works of service, so that the body of Christ may be built up until we all reach unity in the faith and in the knowledge of the Son of God and become mature, attaining to the whole measure of the fullness of Christ.

Ephesians 4:10-13

When I was first appointed a manager in the engineering group of which I was a part, I got into a heated discussion over a technical design with one of my young engineers. In frustration, he finally blurted out, "Well, you have to admit things are as they are!" At the time I thought it a ridiculous argument. Since then I have come to accept it as a profound truth. Things are as they are. You and I are Americans. We are interested in problem-solving and cause and effect and facts. We *do* want answers. So there is something in me that won't let me end our discussion without suggesting a few approaches as to how we might move from being a group of individuals to becoming a company of the committed. What follows is only a beginning, but a journey of a thousand miles starts with the first step. Here are a few first steps.

BEGIN WITH GOD'S WORD

We need to ask ourselves if what this book has presented coincides with what the Holy Spirit is leading us to understand in regard to God's revealed Word for Christians everywhere. If we aren't convicted here, we can't begin. This is not to suggest, however, that we should approach this as an individual assignment or that each person must first become completely convinced as an individual. What better way to understand the mind of the Spirit than to discuss His Word with other believers? This will start us on the road to finding others whom God has prepared to be part of us. For those who are already members of a local church, your church is a natural place to begin (although it may scare some pastors half to death).

Perhaps our initial commitment need only be to spend six weeks with a small group to ask the questions and seek to find answers. Let the Spirit lead. To pastors I would say, preach the word! Invite those in your congregation who respond to such a message to join you in looking at commitment seriously. Perhaps you could take your official board on a weekend retreat to discover "What the Bible says the church should be."

BEGIN WITH A GROUP

Getting a group started is not easy. One of the problems of small groups is their tendency to be stifled by the most reluctant individual or couple (American "fair play"). There are several ways to avoid this. You could ask a number of people to read and discuss this book and to determine whether or not they would like to undertake a journey together. Another book I would suggest is *Creative Love* by Louis Evans Jr. It is a small paperback that discusses "covenant groups" and describes the experiences at the National Presbyterian Church in Washington, D.C. One of the nice things about it is that different chapters explore various dimensions of commitment to one another. It breaks the total down into discussable parts.

If all this sounds like too much to start with, make your own list of things you would like to have as part of a biblical community (see chapter 11) and invite discussion.

This may take some time. One of my problems is that I am always searching for people "like me," people with whom I'll feel comfortable. But if the Bible is true, God has already prepared a local fellowship for each of us. And chances are, as in most local fellowships, there will be a lot of people who will take some getting used to (like me). Right now our local church support group has very few people "like Marge or me." I'm sure many aspects of our everyday life would be completely outside the understanding of some. But we have hung in there through all kinds of life experiences, and we have learned to love one another not because of what we have accomplished or attained but because of who we are *in Christ*.

EXPLORE GIFTS TOGETHER

The most useful tool I have found to help Americans understand and discover their spiritual gifts is Peter Wagner's *Your Spiritual Gifts Can Help Your Church Grow*. The Fuller Evangelistic Association has a series of supplementary workbooks and a leader's guide on discovering spiritual gifts. Although it's quite American in its approach, it is a good place to begin. It not only helps the individual discover his or her gifts, but it is designed so that others will affirm that gift. Wagner's approach is very open-ended. I agree with him that the Bible probably doesn't give a complete list of all spiritual gifts. I also suspect, as does Wagner, that gifts may change from time to time.[1]

What should we expect to find in looking at the spiritual gifts of our group? First, as we noted earlier, we should expect to find someone with the gift of pastor. This may or may not be someone who has gone through seminary, but the Bible never implies that going to seminary is a necessary prerequisite for the pastorate (a rather threatening thought to those of us who have). Second, we should expect to find someone with the gift of teaching. If we don't find anyone with either of those gifts, we should expand our search until we do. To put it another way, God has not yet completed our initial group.

EXPLORING THE FUTURE TOGETHER

What if the ten or twelve or twenty people who decide to make this commitment to one another are already members of an existing church? This is no small dilemma. A key step is discussing the concept with the pastor. To attempt such a fellowship within the context of a larger existing church without the approval of the pastoral staff is impossible and unprofitable. Keep asking. Keep praying. Be patient.

But what if no approval is available? Separation *may be* the answer. But peaceful separation. There is no room for "We have the answer, and you are missing it." Such an attitude can never be the basis of a vital fellowship. Pray a great deal. Take your time. Keep asking one another and the Lord how to communicate your love for those in your present church. If at all possible, ask the church to designate your group, or think of your group as, a new church they have begun.

If, on the other hand, the present leadership is willing to cooperate, two approaches suggest themselves. First, if the Holy Spirit has convicted the pastor that this is God's way, the pulpit will be available to preach and teach what God's Word says a church should be. Again, this takes time. I often suggest that a pastor preach the same sermon six Sundays in a row, using a different outline. I guarantee that on the sixth Sunday someone who has been there for all six weeks will say, "Pastor, I never heard that before!" People change slowly. Let the Holy Spirit do the convicting.[2] (If He wants things speeded up, He'll see to it.)

Next begin the process of exploration. Invite groups to meet together to decide what the Bible says about the church in community. See if some would be willing to participate in a six-month experiment. Perhaps in a church of two hundred, three or four groups of from ten to twenty people would want to try. Plan times for *joint* group sharing as the individual groups are discussing this. After a period of time begin to ask how the present total church might want to change to become what God wants it to become.

As a second approach, let the single group be affirmed by the total church as an experiment. Ask for the church's prayer and emotional support. Wait and see what the Lord does.

This will be much easier for the small church than for the large one because it is much easier to get the support of three hundred than it is of three thousand. But what about a church of three thousand or more members? I have already discussed Wagner's idea of the cell, the congregation, and the celebration. (See page 150.) But that model implies a pastor responsible for each congregation with a "senior pastor" (bishop? overseer? elder?) who is responsible for the smooth functioning of the congregations sharing the same facilities. My American management experience tells me that the best solution is a "matrix" organization. Each pastor would be responsible for his or her congregation, but in addition he or she would have some specialty. It may well be that different congregations within such a "Church at 10th Avenue" may be gifted in special ways. Thus we might find one congregation that has a call to cross-cultural missions. Another might have an emphasis on a ministry of prayer. Still a third might have many with gifts of mercy and want to establish a counseling ministry.[3]

In all of this I am assuming some natural groupings which God in His wisdom has already prepared.[4] Years ago when I was first asked in seminary to attempt to think God's thoughts after Him, I concluded that my task was to attempt to understand God's strategy and to become a part of it. That is what we are attempting here—to become part of God's desire for His church.

God has a future in mind for us. Tomorrow can be better. That's not just an American attribute. That's a *Christian* attribute. There are those who can only see that the world is going to wrack and ruin. Perhaps it is, but that's not the point. God has prepared a new life for us *in Christ*, in His body. And that life is to be lived out in the world *so that the world may know.*

A chorus many of us learned in Sunday school reminds us what a difference one little light can make:

> This little light of mine—
> I'm gonna let it shine.
> This little light of mine—
> I'm gonna let it shine,
> Let it shine, let it shine, let it shine.

During part of the Fourth of July celebration in the Rose Bowl in Pasadena, all the stadium lights are turned off and each person is asked to strike one match. What a beautiful sight it makes!

NOTES

[1]For my own views on this see Edward R. Dayton and David A. Fraser, *Planning Strategies for World Evangelization* (Grand Rapids: Eerdmans, 1979).

[2]See Lyle Schaller, *The Change Agent: The Strategy of Innovative Leadership* (Nashville: Abingdon, 1972). There have been many books written on the dynamics of bringing about change, some better than others, but I like almost everything Lyle Schaller has written. Ted Engstrom and I discuss change in Christian organizations in *Strategy for Leadership.*

[3]See Stephen C. Rose, *The Grass Roots Church* (New York: Holt, Rinehart, and Winston, 1966). Rose suggests that each member commit himself to one particular ministry each year. Such a commitment could be made by each "congregation" in a large church.

[4]In saying this, I do not want to put myself in a predeterminist box and be accused of saying that God has everything worked out ahead of time. Since I, by my very nature, am forced to think in human terms, I cannot be sure how He has it worked out.

CHAPTER 14

Living Life

*Live life, then, with a due sense of responsibility, not as men
who do not know the meaning of life but as those who do.
Make the best use of your time, despite all the evils of these
days.* Ephesians 5:15, 16 PHILLIPS

Living in community as a fellowship of believers is not a
new idea. We are not breaking new ground. Rather, we are
rediscovering what that "cloud of witnesses" discovered
before us. As we have discussed, however, although the
concept is not new, each local fellowship will work out its
community differently. No two communities will be exactly the same because each is responding to a different
society, a different culture, a different set of circumstances.
A community is a response to a situation as well as the
initiation of a new way of living. Therefore, our response to
our American culture will be different from the English
Christians' response to British society and from the
Brazilian Christians' response to Brazilian society.

Today's contemporary communities will not only be
different from other contemporary communities; they also
will be different from the communities of those who have
gone before us, because the church continues to learn
through God's continuing process of revelation. God *is*

doing a new thing, even though it may go by familiar names. It will be different for different groups within the same society. Each situation is unique. Each group of individuals is unique. And the Lord seems to be quite content to allow us our uniquenesses.

Although we cannot know in advance how our community may develop, there are some things we can expect to happen and some lessons we can expect to learn as we attempt to be God's people in a local fellowship. What follows is based both on God's Word and on the experiences of other Christians who have shown us the way.

LEARNING TO TRUST

The world in which we live is not very trustworthy. When individualism is a key value, we can trust no one but ourselves. But when a group of people commit themselves to the Lord and to one another as His church in a specific place in the world, they begin to share their joys, their sorrows, their ups, their downs at an ever-deepening level. It's hard at first. But as we slowly open up to one another, we discover what we really knew all along—that others have problems just as deep as ours. In fact, their problems are often much more serious. Others have the same fears we have. They may be entirely different from ours, but they are still fears.

Trust comes when we discover we can tell another our joys and aches without that person condemning our feelings or trying to solve our problems. Trust comes when we accept others as they are, not as we wish they were. Trust comes when, in an unguarded moment, we reveal part of ourself that we have always kept secret and we find that the other person is just as concerned about keeping our confidence as we are. Trust comes when we sense that another accepts us as we are, not because we have done something wonderful or terrible, not because we are brilliant or witty or beautiful or handsome, but just because we are a person who is loved by the greatest Lover in the world and are a fellow part of His body.

Learning to trust means learning to trust another with our reputation. I have the privilege of serving with four other men as vice presidents of World Vision International. We are "the president's team." We are each quite different. Hal is a West Pointer who was dean of the Army War College. Graeme is an Australian who headed up the YMCA before leading World Vision of Australia. Sam is a native of Madras, India. He is a preacher, a theologian, a thinker. Cliff has a background much like my own, except that he left aerospace to go to seminary ten years younger than I. But we trust each other. More importantly, I trust Hal and Graeme and Sam and Cliff with my reputation and my interests when I am not there. On Tuesday morning when the group meets, one of us will almost always be somewhere else in the world. If I am gone for four weeks, I return confident that these brothers have not forgotten either my opinions nor my interests when they have carried on the business of the organization.

And it is because of trust like this, this acceptance, that Christians can let down the barriers we so quickly erect and allow ourselves to be what we are.

Each of us has three understandings of who we are. We are what *we* think we are. We are what we think others think we are. Lastly, we are what others really think we are. Our heart's desire is to know that others approve of us and *to know they are right*. What a feeling!

LEARNING WHAT IS IMPORTANT

Our culture says that it is what we own that is important. How different from some other cultures. One of my daughters and her husband have been missionaries to a nomadic people called the Turkana in the desert of northern Kenya. In a beautiful book called *Eyelids of the Morning* Alistar Graham and Peter Beard tell the story of landing an airplane among the Turkana for the first time. First, Graham buzzed the people to get their attention. No one even looked up. Then he landed on a flat stretch of sand, expecting to be immediately surrounded by chattering Turkana. No response. Finally, he managed to get one man who apparently was a chief to go for a ride with him. He flew all around Lake Turkana and over the cluster of temporary thatched huts. When he landed, the chief casually walked away and evidently had little to say about the experience. Years later I shared this story with Bedan Mbugua, a Kenyan who was doing research on how to reach the Turkana with the gospel. He told me of a similar experience he had had. When a Land Rover passed the Turkana walking along with their cows and camels and goats, they paid no heed. "Why?" I asked.

"Well," replied Bedan, "the Turkana don't pay any attention to anything unless they know the owner. They value things because of who owns them."

They value things because of the people who own them. We Americans value people because of the things they own. Our materialism tells us that it is how much money we have in the bank or how much power we have or how beautiful we are that is the measure of our worth. Jesus knows that we have need of material things (Matt. 6:32). But he has told us that material things are not worth spending much time thinking about (Matt. 6:25). Once the veneer we wear is chipped away, we can see each other as God sees us, and because He values what He sees, we can value it too. People who live in community stop caring about how rich others are, where they stand in the spiritual pecking order that is so much a part of our Christian society, or even if they are famous in the world's sight.

As we discover that we are accepted by our community for what we are, what the world thinks of us becomes less and less important. The TV commercials for Chevron, Charlie, or Crest, commercials that so often appeal to power, beauty, and wealth, have little attraction. For we are no longer individuals that need to be blown up so the world can see us. Rather, we are part of an organism that is connected to the Lifestream of the world. The world loses its power to set the agenda.

LEARNING TO KNOW MYSELF

If I trust you, if I sense that you have my best interests at heart, then I can hear you when you begin to tell me who I really am. You see, I don't always know who I am. I know what I would like to be. But often I discover that I am not as bad in one area as I thought I was or as good in another area. This is particularly true for me as an American man. My culture has defined for me what I am supposed to be. I am supposed to be strong and confident and self-composed. I am not supposed to cry. When life smacks me in the face with my child's ruptured marriage or the death of a close friend, I am supposed to bully it through with a stiff upper lip. But inside me is a little boy who is often afraid of the world and hurt very badly by failure or disappointment or misunderstanding. I need you to tell me that a man called Jesus wept over the death of his friend Lazarus and over the sin of His nation's capital.

And I have a sneaking suspicion that I am nowhere near as good as I pretend to be or as others say I am. After I had worked as an electronics engineer in the aerospace industry for about eight years, I was part of a team of engineering section heads who were putting together a proposal for a very sophisticated aircraft system. We were working sixty-hour weeks to get it done. It was both exhilarating and exhausting. About halfway through the job we were discussing the instrument display for the pilot. I was asking the others what they thought about part of it. "Ed," commented one of them, "you know more about the display part than all the rest of us. You decide."

I think that was the first time in my engineering career that I heard someone affirm that I really was the expert I was supposed to be. I need others to tell me both who I am and who I am not. But I can only accept the evaluation of people I believe have really had an opportunity to know me.

A real part of knowing myself is knowing my spiritual gifts. I am not as confident as some of my friends are about spiritual gifts. For example, I am not certain about the difference between natural gifts and spiritual gifts. I don't know whether we receive spiritual gifts at the time we become a Christian, or whether God, in His foreknowledge, gave us gifts when we were conceived. I suspect that gifts change with time and that gifts come in response to needs. But I am certain about a few fundamentals, because as I read the Bible, *it* is certain.

First, there are special abilities called "spiritual gifts" or gifts of the Spirit, which each Christian has. Second, these gifts are given to build up the body of Christ, not to enhance the individual believer. Third, these gifts compliment one another in a local fellowship. Fourth, we need to ascertain our gifts and use them for the building up of the body (See page 154 for some further help here.)

But in order to know our gifts we need others to help us identify them and show us how to use them. If we see, for example, that a person has a gift of teaching, then we need to help that person find a teaching position. On the other side of the coin, if we see that a person does not have a gift of hospitality, then we shouldn't ask that person to work in the body in an area where this gift is needed. In other words, we can help others to accept the gifts they have as well as to accept the fact that they don't have others.

And, as we see the gifts of others in the local church, we see that where one is lacking God has made up for it in others. We can accept and know ourselves because we understand that we have a special place in this group. We are not whole without each other. We are not able to function without each other. This makes us able to say, as did my engineering friend, "You're good at that. That's your area of expertise. Why don't you handle it?"

LEARNING TO FIGHT MATERIALISM

Our culture has operated to continually raise our expectations as to what we need. Things that were just wants or "would likes" ten years ago, now have become needs. If we don't have them, something is wrong with us.

Advertising and our consumer society work together to make this happen. One very wealthy man, when asked how much was enough, replied, "Just a little bit more." Consistently over the years surveys have shown that regardless of a person's standard of living, the average person considers that "about twenty percent more" would make him or her content. As long as we define people by what they own, this will be the case. However, when people become more important than things, something interesting begins to happen. We discover that we don't have to hang on as tightly to what is "mine." We begin to see that we don't *need* as many things to define our person as we once did.

Knowing that we are valued as a person sets us free to discard some of the things we thought were needs. We can turn our attention to consciously leveling off and reducing what we own. But we need each other to help us. The early church tried the experiment of having all things in common (Acts 2:44). It created some real tensions, as we read in Acts 6, but the principle was valid in the sense that if all that we call ours as a Christian is really held in stewardship, then we are joint stewards together. It is this sense of joint stewardship that can help us fight back.

Some years ago the Lord really spoke to Marge and me about our standard of living. It wasn't that we were so wealthy. Rather, the Spirit convicted us of our abundance by showing us how poor the rest of the world was. We covenanted together with the Lord to take any additional money we received and give it away. If I got a raise, we would give that away. If someone gave us some money, we would give that away. We opened a separate savings account for the money, realizing that eventually, as inflation overtook us (then at five percent per year!), our standard of living would actually be reduced.

For a few years it worked quite well. Then a financial need came up with one of our children and, after praying about it, we concluded that we should use some of the money to help out. Somehow that broke the covenant, and we have never been able to return to that program. Oh, we continue to increase the percentage of our income that we give each year, but we haven't been able to get back to a standard of negative growth. (Sounds almost un-American, doesn't it?) But I think that with the encouragement of others we could. Certainly what we do with our money is of vital concern to a real community.

In *Rich Christians in an Age of Hunger*, Ron Sider suggests the idea of graduated tithe. The more we earn, the greater the percentage we give. One variation of this is to give just half of whatever increase we get. (We don't even feel it that way.) But I see two important things here: First, we need a compelling reason for giving; and second, we need the community support of others.

Moving from the negative of having too much to the positive of how to have more with less, communities have discovered all kinds of ways to work together, from corporate buying of groceries to sharing garden tools and advice. A logical next step is to divide up the work of living based on the skills within the fellowship, very much like the skills banks that have been appearing recently. After all, if one is a lawyer and one is a carpenter, both can do their specific vocational task better than the other.

Eventually this may free us up for more ministry, which is what happened to the Church of the Redeemer in Houston, Texas.[1] Some of the families took on the task of earning money while others put most of their time into working, much like the paid staff for the church. One could see a community starting with just one couple: "Bill and Ginny, you are really gifted at Christian education. Why don't you go to work for St. John's; the rest of us will pay your salary."

"Time is money," we are told. In our society it certainly is. "Saving time" is an obsession with a lot of us. I have taught a seminar with Ted Engstrom that is called "Managing Your Time." But the title is really just a way of getting you interested. For "managing your time" for the Christian is a question of getting priorities straight.[2] Here again we can expect a close fellowship to help us. Sometimes we need to be *encouraged* not to work. Our culture tells us we need to be busy. Our culture tells us we are lazy if we spend a lot of time doing things other than making money. Our culture tells us we are foolish to help a friend for half a day when we could make fifteen dollars an hour doing our regular job. But those are mostly lies (aren't they?).

LEARNING TO BE ACCOUNTABLE

Oh, oh. Here it comes. Once we commit ourselves to one another, we give others the right to hold us accountable. Chuck Miller used to ask people at the end of a conversation, "How can I pray for you?" Caught unaware, many people would say the first thing that popped into their head. But a week later when Chuck saw the person again, he'd ask, "How did it go?"

"How did *what* go?" was the usual first answer.

"You asked me to pray about your exam. How did it go?"

Chuck held himself accountable to others because he had made a commitment to pray. That not-so-small example tells us something about accountability in a group. First, we are accountable to pray for one another. And in some way the Lord uses that to make us accountable for the other person's welfare. That person, in turn, gives us permission to hold him or her accountable. "Paul, you said you were going to try to spend an extra half hour with the Lord each morning. How is it going?" "Ed, you said you wanted to increase your giving to the Lord to twenty-five percent of your income this year. Did you do it?"

Accountability takes other forms. There is a commitment to a certain time and place. A fellowship must be committed to be together to worship, to learn, to fellowship. "Harold, we missed you and Marion Sunday evening. Where were you?"

Beyond time and place, accountability strengthens us as a group. We become accountable to study a certain passage of Scripture. We become accountable to take our turn at the various worship and service activities. Eventually we become deeply accountable for our very lives as we expect the Spirit to speak to us through the minds and hearts of others.

LEARNING TO REACH OUT

It hurts to be a Christian. If I had said it *costs* to be a Christian, we all would have nodded our heads. Of course it costs. But hurt? I think so. Christians are people who are concerned about the world, and the world is a hurting place.

During the many years I have worked with World Vision I have traveled all over the world, but most of my time has been spent in the "Two-thirds World," the world of "developing nations," the world where the cash income of the average family may be five hundred dollars a year. I must confess that I don't want to see any more of that world. I have gotten to a place where if I never visit another Calcutta slum or another village full of hungry people, that will be fine. Every time I board an airplane heading overseas, I get numb inside. I can't bear to watch the TV specials that World Vision uses to tell the story of the world's needs. When you have been there, it is too real, at least for me.

The Spirit sensitizes us to need, and He does it very often through one another. Often the need is not what we imagined it would be. Isn't it interesting how little the New Testament has to say about evangelism? Paul uses the word only three times. As Karl Barth points out in his commentary on Romans, after eleven chapters of reasoned doctrine we would expect Paul to start talking about going out and telling people about Jesus. But what does Romans 12 talk about? People. Relationships. Justice. Mercy. Love. When we love one another in the power of Jesus Christ, we *naturally* want to share that love with others. The young church didn't have to be told how to *do* evangelism. All it had to do was *be* itself and to do what was natural. What could be more attractive to today's American than to see a group of people who obviously care more about one another than they do about wealth and power, who accept one another as they are, who live lives as families that demonstrate concern and honor one another.

But a concern for the world goes beyond attracting others by what we are. Concern for the world is active. It discovers needs and seeks to have a part in God's answer for them. Some are close. Some are overseas. In the midst of our affluent society live millions of hungry (American) people. Those of us in the American middle-class know very little about them. We really don't want to know. But they are there. They are those who couldn't "make it" in America. Take any urban area in the United States and draw a circle with a one-mile radius. Inside that circle you will find hundreds of very poor, hurting people.

Widen that circle to include the Two-Thirds World and the number of hurting people becomes millions. In both places there is not only physical hunger, there is spiritual starvation. Some members of our community may have to be set aside, much as were Paul and Barnabas in Acts 13, for the work to which the Holy Spirit has called them. That's not easy. That hurts. It hurts to have your children leave to serve the Lord in hard places. It hurts to be there yourself.

But that can happen when a group of people commit themselves to untie the cultural ropes that immobilize them.

LEARNING ABOUT MARRIAGE

If I were going to write another book on Christian commitment, a book that didn't attempt to focus on the hindrances of culture, as this one does, I would begin with marriage. The commitment of a man and a woman in marriage is such a high commitment, such a unique commitment, that Paul compares it to the relationship of Christ to the Church (Eph. 5:21ff). Our society has produced a lot of myths about marriage, but they all boil down to one idea: the individual is more important than the couple. If I can't get along with you, if you bug me to death, if I don't find you attractive anymore, if I find someone else who is more appealing to me, if you don't seem to understand me . . . whatever. If any of these things is true, then the best thing for *me* is to get out.

But Christians also have a few myths about marriage. One of them is that there is one perfect mate for each of us and that we need to find just that person. At first glance, that seems all right, or at least harmless. After all, if God is in control, He has already picked out the person for me. Right? Well, not quite. That puts all the responsibility on God and takes away our freedom. It removes the mystery, the paradox of God's will and human freedom. God's Word has very little to say about how to find a mate, but it has much to say about keeping one. Who does God want us to be married to? The person we are married to right now. What kind of marriage will be "successful"? One that is based on a mutual commitment to Christ and a commitment to one another based on His Word. Christ has said to His church that He will never let us go. His commitment is irrevocable. That's the model Ephesians 5 uses for husbands and wives.

What has this to do with a local fellowship? First, the local fellowship can model for us the kind of commitment that Christians are to have to one another. Second, the local fellowship can train us as to what Christian marriage should be like so we understand the nature of the commitment before we enter into it. Third, the local fellowship can encourage us in the commitments we have already made as husbands and wives. When a Christian marriage fails, the church has failed.

LEARNING TO ACCOMMODATE FAMILIES

Marge and I began our family with three girls who were all born within three years of one another. We had some strong ideas of our own about how to raise children, and we also received guidance and encouragement from our local fellowship.

When the youngest was two, our pastor's wife informed us that the girls were old enough to be in church on Sunday morning; so each Sunday we partially filled up the third pew on the left-hand side. The girls were supposed to pay attention until the sermon began, at which time they could get out their coloring books. (When we moved from the East Coast to Grand Rapids we discovered that coloring in church was sinful, but that eating candy was all right.) I think we went through four different Bible story books. Jill says they helped her get *A*'s in Bible at college.

But when Rob came along, thirteen years after our youngest girl, it was a new ball game. To begin with, according to his grandfather, he had four mothers. But beyond that, the things we did naturally as young parents, things that were strongly reinforced by our local church back East, came a lot harder out here in Southern California. For example, someone decided we would no longer have memory work in Sunday school. (Something about it not being good to force anyone to memorize things they didn't understand.) So we haven't had the same encouragement with Rob, and I think he has missed something because of it. (But how blessed we are by all he is doing to be Christ's man in his high school today!)

The local fellowship is meant to be a family affair. The larger it gets the greater its tendency to split off the young people into "youth groups." We should expect a local fellowship to be a place where children feel at home, but it should especially be a place of common understanding as to right and wrong. Living in a very wealthy, very worldly city, we find we need the counterbalance of a Christian community that has standards about rightness and wrongness. How often are you bombarded with, "Gee, Mom, the Walkers let Jimmy stay out until eleven"? Communities have a way of setting community standards, standards that young people desperately need.

LEARNING TO MOVE DEEPER INTO CHRIST

One of the apostle Paul's favorite expressions is "in Christ." He wants to be found in Christ, to live in Christ, to be loved in Christ. But to be in Christ is to be "in" His body, the church. To know Him better, to experience Him more deeply, more fully, is to experience others that same way. And it means to suffer in Christ, to share in His suffering. Part of that suffering involves the hurts of human relationships. It hurts to see friends lose their children in an automobile accident. It hurts to have others let us down. It hurts to be misunderstood. It hurts to be honest with one another. It hurts to be vulnerable.

When I was a young Christian I thought that as I grew older, more mature, I would grow closer and closer to Him. I pictured a graph with closeness to God measured vertically and time measured horizontally. I anticipated that as I got rid of some of my sins, as I got to know His Word better, as I worshiped more, the dot representing me would gradually rise on the graph. Oh, I didn't expect to ever reach His level, just get closer.

What I have discovered is that the older I get and the more I come to *know* God, the more awesome and impossibly wonderful He becomes. Yes, I've cleaned up my act. I have left many of my sins behind me. I am a better person than I was forty years ago. But my understanding of who God *is* has magnified a hundred times. He has moved right off the top of the graph. Now I know that there is more to Him than I will ever comprehend or apprehend.

Community is like that. There is always more because there is always more of Christ.

NOTES

[1]See Michael Harper, *A New Way of Living* (Plainfield: Logos, 1973).

[2]See Edward R. Dayton and Ted W. Engstrom, *Strategy for Living: How to Make the Best Use of Your Time and Abilities* (Glendale: Regal, 1976).

PART 4

An Optimistic Epilogue

CHAPTER 15

What of Tomorrow?

No, in all these things we are more than conquerors through him who loved us. For I am convinced that neither death nor life, neither angels nor demons, neither the present nor the future, nor any powers, neither height nor depth, nor anything else in all creation, will be able to separate us from the love of God that is in Christ Jesus our Lord. Romans 8:37–39

Christians stand in two kingdoms—a kingdom that has arrived and a kingdom that is yet to come. We believe in a blessed hope. We have a straight-line view of history that culminates in a new heaven and a new earth. We look forward to the return of our Lord and Savior. We are basically optimistic people.

Yet at the same time, we live with tension. At best, the Bible gives only a little indication that this kingdom will become all it should be before the return of Christ. And, at the worst, it indicates that we may actually go through a considerable amount of tribulation before Christ's return.

Truly we live in an upside-down kingdom. Why should the poor be blessed? And why should the poor, the peacemakers, the people who thirst after righteousness, be persecuted (Matt. 5:9)?

We are heirs of the kingdom, joint heirs with Christ, and

yet there is that catch, "*if. . . we share in his sufferings. . . .*" (Rom. 8:17).

We are called to attempt to counter the results of the Fall, even while understanding that only when the coming kingdom has completely arrived and Christ is seated at the right hand of the Father will the lion lie down with the lamb (Heb. 12:2).

HOW SHALL WE LIVE?

Some say there is not much we can do about the world. It is obviously going from bad to worse. All the trouble and turmoil that surrounds us are signs of the "last days," we are told. We can almost feel a sense of rejoicing that these *are* the last days and that we, consequently, will be removed from all responsibility. We are like Hezekiah, who, when told that disaster would not strike until the reign of his son, turned to the wall and smiled (2 Kings 20:19).

It has been so ever since. The writers of the New Testament obviously felt they were living in the last days, as did many who followed them down the paths of history. During the unbelievable years of fourteenth-century Europe, the continent was decimated by the Black Plague and by continuous warfare. If we had been alive to witness the deaths of the thousands of victims of the plague, or if we had lived during a time when roving bands of independent armies fought each other, as was true in the fourteenth century, would not we have believed we were indeed living in the last days?[1]

The concept of the last days is given to us not so we can revel in prophecy, not so we can retreat from the world, but so we can understand how to live. Fundamental to the biblical concept of living is that there is a new life, a new life *in Christ*, and that to be in Christ is to be in one another.

Are we in the last days? Certainly. Is the Apocalypse at the door? Certainly. It has always been "Apocalypse Now." Are things about to get much worse? Perhaps. Are things about to get much better? Perhaps. But we are not responsible for what God is going to do or what He will permit in the future. We are responsible for living now.

We could well be in the midst of what some have termed the Third Great Awakening. Richard Lovelace picks up this theme in quoting C.C. Cole's view that the first two Great Awakenings shared a discernible pattern. Both began with widespread grass-roots evangelism.

> This was followed by five subsequent phases of development in a regular pattern of succession: (1) the organization of home and foreign mission societies to channel new leadership into church planting or into the field; (2) the production and distribution of Christian literature; (3) the renewal and extension of Christian education institutions; (4) attempts at "the reformation of manners"—i.e., the reassertion of Christian moral standards in a decadent society; and (5) the great humanitarian crusades against social evils like slavery, war and intemperance.[2]

We must be careful at this point not to fall prey to the American penchant for asking about cause and effect; we cannot expect that since the first three are here, the others will follow. Everything good is of God. It may be that the culture has come to the end of itself and created a climate within which the Holy Spirit may work. It may be that the Holy Spirit is operating against society, crying out with Jonah, "Destruction is at hand. Repent!"

History is replete with movement and countermovement, with action and reaction. It has something to do with the cycle of generations. Perhaps it has something to do with the inherent rebellion found in humanity, a rebellion in which humanity seeks to find its own way independent from the way of its parents. The promiscuity of the seventeenth century was replaced by the Victorian morality of the nineteenth, and so on.

Within the evangelical camp some see a dangerous weakening of the evangelical conviction. Their key issue is the question of "biblical inerrancy." They essentially hold a domino theory that assumes that once we give up our belief in the scientific factualness of God's Word (as given in the original manuscripts), we soon lose the authority of God's Word and thus remove ourselves from under the authority of God.

But others see that this indeed may be the beginning of a Holy Spirit motivated revival. We may not agree with the methods of the Moral Majority, but we have to admit that they are attempting to do something about our society.

It is interesting to compare what the secularists and the Christians are saying about the condition of our times and about the meaning of what is happening.

SECULAR SOCIETY EXAMINES ITSELF

Daniel Yankelovich believes that "tomorrow is not going to be like yesterday." He sees a cultural revolution, which, though it will speak out against the self-fulfillment movement, will turn out quite differently. He agrees with Daniel Bell that "our culture and our economy are on opposite courses: while the culture calls for freedom, the economy calls for constraint."[3]

In 1970 Charles Reich saw a brave new world rising out of the ashes of the post-Vietnam rebellion of American youth. He talked about the *Greening of America*. He saw a new consciousness arising, in some inexplicable way, after what might be viewed as an anarchist attempt to destroy an old culture so a new one could be built. How this was to happen he was not able to say. He talked about a third level of consciousness that would somehow break down the confining structures of society.[4]

Ten years later, Alvin Toffler wrote about a *Third Wave*, a tidal wave of changes in history. For Toffler the first wave was launched by the agricultural revolution and the second by the industrial revolution. Toffler believes the Third Wave will create a new civilization in our midst with its own jobs, lifestyles, work ethic, sexual attitudes, concepts of life, economic structures, and political mindedness. The blurb on Toffler's book jacket says, "startling in concept, written with extraordinary clarity and perception, the *Third Wave* prepares us to cope with the future that is already here."[5] Yet the author really never explains how all of this is to happen.

In the *Aquarian Conspiracy: Personal and Social Transformation in the 1980s*, Marilyn Ferguson sees a "great shuddering, irrevocable shift overtaking us." For Ferguson it's not a new political system nor a new religious system nor a new economic system. "It is a new mind—a turnabout in consciousness in critical members of individuals, a network powerful enough to bring about radical change in our culture."[6] Amazingly, Ferguson ranges over the breadth and width of the cultural changes taking place as result of increased communication without ever attributing any Godward dimension to all of this. She even quotes C. S. Lewis without acknowledging his religious (and very Christian) beginning point.

Ferguson also quotes De Tocqueville: "Time, events, or the unaided individual action of the mind will sometimes undermine or destroy an opinion without any outward sign of change . . . no conspiracy has been formed to make war on that [opinion], but its followers one-by-one noiselessly succeed. As its opponents remain mute or only interchange their thoughts by stealth, they themselves remain unaware for a long period that a great revolution has actually been affected."[7]

I would argue that the revolution De Tocqueville talked about and the one Ferguson is referring to are two different revolutions.

For some secularists there is hope. In a 1980 article on capitalism entitled "A Revolution of Self-love," *Time* magazine enjoins and quotes economist Robert Heilbroener, "one of capitalism's most fervent critics and an advocate of central economic planning," as saying, "History has shown capitalism to be an extraordinarily resilient, persistent, tenacious system, perhaps because its driving force is dispersed among so much of its population rather than concentrated solely in a governing elite." *Time* then concludes, "after predicting its [capitalism's] imminent collapse for well over a century, even capitalism's critics recognize the staying powers of its ideas."[8]

And yet, in a later issue, *Time* admitted there is a need to "revive responsibility." Says *Time*, "Armed with the knowledge that they are not *fated to succeed* [italics mine], Americans can take up the complicated burden of choosing to succeed, of making their way creatively across the expanses of their possibilities. That venture could be as liberating to the national spirit as the first forays west across the mountains."[9]

While some secular optimists look toward a future with anticipation and excitement, others wonder whether we will survive the "challenges of the 80s."[10] In an interview in *Quest* magazine in October 1979, Richard Russell comments: "The government has gotten away from the old Puritan ethic of debt being basically dangerous. In 1929 the federal debt was about sixteen billion. Since then the population has doubled, but the debts have gone up to 800 billion. We're building federal debt at the rate of two billion a month. . . . People believe that you can always sell what you bought to somebody else for a higher price. But there comes a point when the last item is sold to the last buyer and that's it."[11]

Russell's concern is amplified by the Club of Rome's study on *Limits to Growth*. No matter how we reorganize the variety of ecology, energy, and bodies in the computer, it always predicts disaster.

CHRISTIAN SOCIETY EXAMINES ITSELF

But what of Lovelace's and Cole's view that we may be in the midst of a Third Great Awakening? How do Christians view themselves? Lovelace wonders whether evangelicals are truly attempting "the reformation of manners" so necessary. He also wonders whether evangelicals have awakened to their sense of responsibility to stand over and against the world.

Judging from evangelical experience in the nineteenth century, some degree of activity and some sense of responsibility for action are necessary if Christians are to be the level of society that promotes justice, and the salt that inhibits decay. It also seems clear that *uninstructed Christians will not automatically develop these qualities* [italics mine], especially if they are embedded in socially and passive churches. Born again souls do not necessarily have born again minds—as we have discovered in the phenomenon of fundamentalist racism. Regeneration must be continued through growth and sanctification; new Christians must be reformed by the renewal of their minds.[12]

But can we not see some awakening among evangelicals in terms of social concern? In 1967 when I completed seminary (as part of my mid-life crisis!) and planned to work jointly with Fuller School of World Mission and World Vision International, I was told that World Vision International was collecting money from evangelicals to support orphans, money that should rightfully be used for preaching the gospel. Today the World Vision International partnership, which includes ten Western countries and reaches out to over eighty non-Western countries, is one of the largest Christian organizations in the world, and "Christian development" is not only respectable but very much a major part of Christian thinking. Television has brought the hurt of the world into the living rooms of America, and Christians have responded as we hoped they would.

Evangelicals are beginning to vigorously question America's disproportionate consumption of the world's material resources. Evangelicals for Social Action is a growing force. Ron Sider's *Rich Christians in an Age of Hunger* has gained popular acceptance if not popular response. Stan Mooneyham's *What Do You Say to a Hungry World?* has sharpened evangelical sensitivity. Tom Sine's *The Mustard Seed Conspiracy* sets forth some creative responses.

Out of the ashes of Watergate has come Chuck Colson's prison ministry.[13] A man who exemplified everything that was vilified by the American press was born again.[14] The result was not only an individual transformation, but a commitment to a ministry within prisons that is undergirded by a close fellowship of believers.

In 1970 John Perkins, who had moved to Mendenhall, Mississippi, to try to help black families there, was nearly beaten to death by Mississippi sheriffs. In 1980 he was voted one of the Outstanding Men of the Decade by the state of Mississippi. The ministry of the Voice of Calvary is demonstrating that Christians can and do bridge racial distinctions that are deeply embedded in the culture.[15]

In analyzing a series of surveys conducted over the past five years, George Gallup discovered a number of encouraging trends. He found youth yearning for a solid foundation as opposed to a superficial Christianity. During a time when we have come to believe that the American family is disintegrating at an ever-increasing rate, Gallup discovered that the percentage of adults who say they are *satisfied* with their family life has increased over the last five years. At the same time, Gallup finds a nationwide acceptance of traditional values among both the churched and the unchurched!

- Nine out of ten (89%) say they would welcome more respect and authority in the coming years.
- A similar proportion (91%) would welcome more emphasis on traditional family ties.
- Seven out of ten (69%) say they would welcome more emphasis on working hard.
- Three out of four (74%) would *not like* to see more acceptance of marijuana usage, and six out of ten (62%) would be opposed to wider acceptance of sexual freedom.[16]

Finally, Gallup and others have discovered that the clergy in America are much more conservative than one would imagine and that the younger clergy are much more traditional in their views than many have thought.

In the movement toward becoming involved in the physical and social hurts of the world, evangelicals appear to be recapturing, to some degree, an understanding that the kingdom of God as proclaimed by our Lord includes not only preaching but "healing and casting out demons" (Matt. 10:1).

Missions historian Ralph Winter, along with others we have mentioned, also sees a third era—a Third Era of Missions.[17] The first surge of activity in the early nineteenth century reached the untouched nations of the world; the Second Era moved inland (Africa *Inland* Mission, Sudan *Interior* Mission, China *Inland* Mission); and Winter sees us now in the Third (perhaps final) Era of reaching the "Hidden People," the thousands of unreached people groups that are scattered among the nation states of the world.[18]

The new awakening on the part of young people to the need for and the potential of communicating Christ all over the world certainly is cause for optimism. Youth With a Mission (YWAM), now with a permanent staff of over two thousand spread around the world, is a vehicle through which over ten thousand young people are discovering what it means to reach out in simple faith to do the impossible. The most recent statistics on the total number of North American missionaries show the number of "short termers" has grown from 5,764 in 1975 to 17,633 in 1979.

During the period from 1975 to 1979, ninety-four new mission agencies were formed, increasing the total from 620 in 1975 to 714 in 1979. During the nineteenth century, the gospel circled the globe. William Carey, the "Father of Modern Missions," estimated in 1793[19] that less than one-third of the nation-states of the world had any Christian witness. By the turn of the century, Christians were found in every country of the world. Today, these "second generation" churches are reaching out to announce the kingdom to others around the world.[20] They are also helping us in the West to see the possibility of living as those who are mysteriously and organically related to one another in the body of Christ.

Lane Dennis believes there is *A Reason for Hope* and that the church has a golden opportunity now to recover the real task of its calling.[21] He calls on us to put complete trust in Christian ideals, in the Bible, and in biblical teaching.

Jeremey Rifkin believes there is an *Emerging Order,* which is how Christians will live in an age of scarcity. Rifkin feels that the tremendous growth of the evangelical movement, combined with the dynamism of Pentecostal-ism, must produce a new society.[22]

But neither Dennis nor Rifkin is able to go much beyond Charles Reich or Marilyn Ferguson in explaining how all of this will happen. Perhaps rightfully so. How audacious it would be for us to assert with certainty what God is about to do!

Americans are desperately searching for community. Certainly they should be able to find it within the local church. One by one we have peeled away the layers of our individualism only to discover there is no core, there is no "self" inside. I exist only as you exist. I love only if you are there to be loved.

Much of the current despair in America is despair over "The System." No one is quite sure what The System is, but it's something that is no longer under any human control. It has been given a life by some mysterious "they." The System drives people to acts of violence. The System leaves people feeling they have to "go along" to get ahead in the world. The System seeks to control our lives and robs us of freedom of expression and freedom of choice, particularly choice as to relationships. The System dictates where we will work, how we will live, what clothes we will wear, what gadgets we must have in our homes.

But throughout America we detect attempts to bring people into relationship and to stand over and against such a system. Consumers Union, Common Cause, The Moral Majority, and The Neighborhood Crime Watch all are testimonies to the fact that we are crying out, "I need *your help*. I can't go it alone."

We, as Christians, know that The System is that worldly system dominated by Satan. And, at a much deeper level, we are coming to understand that we are not contending with flesh and blood, but that we are wrestling with the spiritual powers of darkness (Eph. 6:12). "And we can't go it alone."

THE CALL TO COMMITMENT

To imply that during its "better years" the church had a more profound understanding of the type of community advocated in this book would be inaccurate and unfair. There have always been both sedentary and "set apart" groups of Christians that were committed to one another. The bands of twelve that left Ireland to evangelize Europe in the seventh century, the Roman Catholic orders, the beautiful communities that were built around the cathedrals of the twelfth century are all evidence of this type of community. The major difference was that most of these communities had analogies within their cultures. The tribe, the family, the allegiance to the larger group were all part of most cultures of the world. The relationships that existed or were expected between people were often quite similar to those the Bible describes.

But in this day, in this culture, we no longer have those models, and somehow we must reconstruct them in order to recapture not only what we have lost as Christians, but what our culture has lost.

COMMITMENT IS COMMUNITY

God has called us to come out of ourselves and to be "in Christ." To be in Christ means to be members of one another. In this day, in this age, in this nation—indeed, in this culture—the model of what can happen when people become committed to one another through the power of the Holy Spirit is a model the world longs to see. Let's discover it together.

NOTES

[1]When Barbara W. Tuchman's striking history of the fourteenth century, *A Distant Mirror: The Calamitous Fourteenth Century* (New York: Knopf, 1978), was first released, my wife asked me why I was plowing through it night after night. "It gives me hope," I replied. "I can't believe anything could *ever* be this bad again."

[2]Richard Lovelace, "Completing an Awakening," *Christian Century*, March 1981, 296.

[3]Daniel Yankelovitch, "New Rules in American Life: Searching for Self-Fulfillment in a World Turned Upside Down," *Psychology Today*, April 1981,   35. Also see his book *New Rules* (New York: Random House, 1981).

[4]See Charles A. Reich, *Greening of America: How the Youth Revolution Is Trying to Make America Liveable* (New York: Random House, 1970).

[5]See Alvin Toffler, *The Third Wave* (New York: Morrow, 1980).

[6]See Marilyn Ferguson, *The Aquarian Conspiracy: Personal and Social Transformation in the 1980s* (Los Angeles: J. P. Tarcher, 1981). It is interesting that some commentaries are now labeling this "conspiracy" as part of a new counter-Christian religion known as "New Age."

[7]Ibid.,   195.

[8]"A Revolution of Self-love," *Time*, April 21, 1980,   45.

[9]"Needed: Individual Awareness and a Sense of Nationhood," *Time*, February 23, 1981,   72.

[10]"Special Report," *U.S. News and World Report*, October 15, 1979.

[11]Richard Russell, *Quest*, October 1979.

[12]Richard Lovelace, "Completing an Awakening,"   296.

[13]See Charles Colson, *Life Sentence* (Lincoln: Chosen, 1979).

[14]See Charles Colson, *Born Again* (New York: Bantam, 1976).

[15]See John Perkins, *Let Justice Roll Down* (Glendale: Regal, 1976).

[16]See George Gallup, Jr. and David Poling, *The Search for America's Faith*, (Nashville: Abingdon, 1980).

[17]"The Concept of a Third Era of Missions," *Evangelical Quarterly*, April 1981, 69.

[18]For a deeper understanding of the depth and breadth of this task, see *Unreached Peoples*, published annually since 1979 by David C. Cook, edited by C. Peter Wagner, Edward R. Dayton, and Samuel Wilson.

[19]See William Carey, *An Inquiry into the Obligation of Christians to Use Means for the Conversion of the Heathen.* A facsimile of the 1792 edition is available from Carey Kingsgate Press, London.

[20]Ted Engstrom has painted a positive picture of the future of missions in his book *What in the World Is God Doing? The New Face of Missions* (Waco: Word, 1978).

[21]See Lane Dennis, *A Reason for Hope*, (Old Tappan: Revell, 1976).

[22]See Jeremy Rifkin and Ted Howard, *The Emerging Order: God in the Age of Scarcity* (New York: Putnam, 1979).

Bibliography

Anderson, Courtney. *To the Golden Shore: The Life of Adoniram Judson.* Boston: Little, Brown, 1956.

Armstrong, Ben. *The Electric Church.* Nashville: Nelson, 1979.

Augustine, Saint. *City of God.* New York: Doubleday, 1957.

Barnet, Richard J. and Ronald E. Muller. *Global Reach: The Power of the Multinational Corporation.* New York: Simon & Schuster, 1974.

Bauer, P.T. *Dissertation on Development.* Cambridge: Harvard University Press, 1971.

Becker, Ernest. *Denial of Death.* New York: Free Press, 1973.

Bell, Daniel. *The Cultural Contradictions of Capitalism.* New York: Basic, 1976.

Bellah, Robert N. *The Broken Covenant: American Civil Religion in Time of Trial.* New York: Seabury, 1976.

Bennis, Waren G., and Philip E. Slater. *The Temporary Society.* New York: Harper and Row, 1968.

Berger, Peter L. *Facing Up to Modernity: Excursions in Sociology, Politics, and Religion.* New York: Basic, 1979.

_____. *The Heretical Imperative: Contemporary Possibilities of Religious Affirmation.* New York: Doubleday, 1976.

_____. *Pyramids of Sacrifice: Political Ethics and Social Change.* New York: Doubleday, 1976.

Berger, Peter L., et al. *Homeless Mind: Modernization and Consciousness.* New York: Irvington, 1973.

Berger, Peter L., and Thomas Luckmann. *The Social Construction of Reality.* New York: Doubleday, 1967.

217

Berger, Peter L., and Richard J. Neuhaus. *Against the World for the World.* New York: Seabury, 1976.

Bloesch, Donald G. *The Evangelical Renaissance.* Grand Rapids: Eerdmans, 1973.

Boetger, Gary. *In Search of Balance.* Roslyn Heights: Libra, 1976.

Bonhoeffer, Dietrich. *The Cost of Discipleship.* New York: Macmillan, 1963.

———. *Letters and Papers from Prison.* New York: Macmillan, 1953.

Brandt, Willy, and Anthony Sampson, eds. *North-South: A Program for Survival.* Cambridge: MIT Press, 1980.

Bright, John. *The Kingdom of God.* Nashville: Abingdon, 1953.

Bronwell, Arthur B., ed. *Science and Technology in the World of the Future.* New York: John Wiley & Sons, 1970.

Brown, Harold O. J. *Christianity and the Class Struggle.* Grand Rapids: Zondervan, 1970.

Bunyan, John. *Pilgrim's Progress.* New York: Lighthouse, 1976.

Burdick, Eugene, and William J. Lederer. *The Ugly American.* New York: Norton, 1958.

Calvin, John. *Institutes of the Christian Religion: Beveridge Translation.* Volume III. Grand Rapids: Eerdmans, 1953.

Carey, William. *An Inquiry Into the Obilgation of Christians to Use Means for the Conversion of the Heathen.* A facsimile of the 1792 edition is available from Carey Kingsgate Press, London.

Carnell, Edward John. *The Case for Orthodox Theology.* Philadelphia: Westminster, 1959.

———. *Christian Commitment.* New York: Macmillan, 1957.

Clouse, Robert G., et al. *The Cross and the Flag.* Carol Stream: Creation House, 1972.

Colson, Charles W. *Born Again.* New York: Bantam, 1976.

———. *Life Sentence.* Lincoln: Chosen, 1979.

Costas, Orlando E. *The Church and Its Mission: A Shattering Critique from the Third World.* Wheaton: Tyndale, 1975.

Dayton, Donald W. *Discovering an Evangelical Heritage.* New York: Harper and Row, 1976.

Dayton, Edward R., ed. *Mission Handbook.* Eleventh edition. Monrovia: MARC, 1977.

———. *God's Purpose/Man's Plans.* Monrovia, MARC, 1971.

———. *That Everyone May Hear.* Third edition. Monrovia, MARC, 1983.

———. *Tools for Time Management.* Revised edition. Grand Rapids: Zondervan, 1983.

Dayton, Edward R., and Ted W. Engstrom. *Strategy for Living: How to Make the Best Use of Your Time and Abilities.* Glendale: Regal, 1976.

———. *Strategy for Leadership.* Old Tappan: Revell, 1978.

Dayton, Edward R., and David A Fraser. *Planning Strategies For World Evangelization.* Grand Rapids: Eerdmans, 1979.

Dean, John. *Blind Ambition: The White House Years.* New York: Simon and Schuster, Inc., 1976.

Dennis, Lane. *A Reason For Hope.* Old Tappan: Revell, 1976.

de Tocqueville, Alexis. *Democracy in America.* Edited by Richard O. Heffner. New York: The New American Library, 1956.

Dobson, James. *Hide or Seek.* Old Tappan: Revell, 1974.

Donovan, Vincent J. *Christianity Rediscovered,* rev. ed. Maryknoll: Orbis, 1982.

Douglas, J. D., ed. *Let the Earth Hear His Voice.* Minneapolis: World Wide Publications, 1975.

Drucker, Peter. *Adventures of a Bystander.* New York: Harper and Row, 1979.

_____. *The Age of Discontinuity.* New York: Harper and Row, 1969.

Edwards, Jonathan. *The Works of President Edwards.* Vol. 4. Edited by Edward Williams and Edward Parsons. New York: Burt Franklin, 1968.

Ellul, Jacques. *Hope in Time of Abandonment.* New York: Seabury, 1978.

_____. *Technological Society.* New York: Random House, 1967.

Engstrom, Ted W. *What in the World is God Doing? The New Face of Missions.* Waco: Word, 1978.

Engstrom, Ted W. and Edward R. Dayton. *Strategy for Leadership.* Old Tappan: Revell, 1979.

Engstrom, Ted W., and David J. Juroe. *The Work Trap.* Old Tappan: Revell, 1979.

Evans, Louis H. *Creative Love.* New York: Fawcett, 1979.

Fairlie, Henry. *The Seven Deadly Sins Today.* Washington: New Republic, 1978.

Ferguson, Marilyn. *The Aquarian Conspiracy: Personal and Social Transformation in the 1980s.* Los Angeles: J. P. Tarcher, 1981.

Fischer, David Hackett. *Growing Old in America.* New York: Oxford University Press, 1978.

Fizgerald, Frances. *America Revised.* Boston: Little, Brown, 1979.

Florovsky, Georges. *Christianity and Culture.* Belmont: Nordland, 1974.

Foster, George M. *Traditional Cultures and the Impact of Technological Change.* New York: Harper and Row, 1962.

Foster, Richard J. *Celebration of Discipline: Paths to Spiritual Growth.* New York: Harper and Row, 1978.

Freire, Paulo. *Pedagogy of the Oppressed.* New York: Seabury, 1970.

Friesen, Garry. *Decision Making and the Will of God.* Portland: Multnomah, 1980.

Gallup, George Jr., and David Poling. *The Search for America's Faith.* Nashville: Abingdon, 1980.

Gardner, John W. *Excellence: Can We Be Equal and Excellent Too?* New York: Harper and Row, 1971.

Getz, Gene A. *Sharpening the Focus of the Church*. Chicago: Moody, 1976.

Goodwin, Richard. *The American Condition*. New York: Doubleday, 1974.

Greeley, Andrew M. *Why Can't They Be Like Us? America's White Ethnic Groups*. New York: Dutton, 1971.

Green, Michael. *Evangelism in the Early Church*. Grand Rapids: Eerdmans, 1970.

Greenleaf, Robert K. *Servant Leadership: A Journey into the Nature of Power and Greatness*. New York: Paulist Press, 1977.

Gross, Martin. *The Pyschological Society*. New York: Random House, 1978.

Halberstam, David. *The Best and the Brightest*. New York: Random House, 1972.

Hall, Brian P. *Value Clarifications As Learning Process: A Guidebook for Educators*. New York: Paulist Press, 1974.

Harper, Michael. *A New Way of Living*. Plainfield: Logos, 1973.

Harrington, Michael. *The Other America: Poverty in the United States*. Baltimore: Penguin, 1963.

Hatfield, Mark. *Between a Rock and a Hard Place*. Waco: Word, 1977.

Heilbroner, Robert L., and Aaron Singer. *The Economic Transformation of America*. New York: Harcourt Brace Jovanovich, 1977.

Henderson, Hazel. *Creating Alternative Futures*. New York: Perigee, 1978.

Henry, Carl F.H. *Evangelicals in Search of Identity*. Waco: Word, 1976.

Herzberg, Frederick. *Work and the Nature of Man*. New York: Crowell, 1966.

Howe, Leland W., et al. *Values Clarification*. New York: Hart, 1972.

Johnson, Warren. *Muddling Toward Frugality*. Niwot: Sierra Publications, 1978.

Jones, E. Stanley. *The Unshakable Kingdom and the Unchanging Person*. Nashville: Abingdon, 1972.

Kahn, Herman. *World Economic Development*. Boulder: Westview, 1979.

Kenniston, Kenneth, and the Carnegie Council on Children. *All Our Children*. New York: Harcourt Brace Jovanovich, 1977.

Kennedy, Gerald. *The Lion and the Lamb: Paradoxes of the Christian Faith*. New York: Abingdon, 1950.

Kennedy, James D. *Evangelism Explosion*. Wheaton: Tyndale, 1970.

Kiev, Air. *A Strategy for Daily Living*. New York: Free Press, 1973.

Kirschenbaum, Howard, et al. *Values Clarification*. New York: Hart, 1972.

Kraus, C. Norman. *The Community of the Spirit*. Grand Rapids: Eerdmans, 1973

Kraybill, Donald B. *The Upside Down Kingdom*. Scottsdale: Herald Press, 1978.

Kubler-Ross, Elizabeth. *Questions and Answers on Death and Dying*. New York: Macmillan, 1974.

Kuhn, Thomas S. *The Structure of Scientific Revolutions* (Volume II, No. 2). Chicago: University of Chicago Press, 1970.

Ladd, George E. *The Gospel of the Kingdom*. Grand Rapids: Wm. B. Eerdmans, 1959.

Larson, Roland S., and Doris E. Larson. *Values and Faith: Value Clarifying Exercises for Family and Church Groups*. Minneapolis: Winston Press, 1976.

Lasch, Christopher. *The Culture of Narcissim: American Life in an Age of Diminishing Expectations*. New York: Norton, 1979.

Lausanne Committee for World Evangelism. *Lausanne Occasional Papers, No. 2: The Willowbank Report—Gospel and Culture*. Wheaton: Lausanne Committee for World Evangelism, 1978.

Lederer, William J., and Eugene Burdick. *The Ugly American*. New York: Norton, 1958.

Lewis, C.S. *Four Loves*. New York: Harcourt Brace Jovanovich, 1971.

Lindsell, Harold. *Battle for the Bible*. Grand Rapids: Zondervan, 1978.

Locke, John. *Two Treatises of Government*. London: Cambridge University Press, 1967.

Mander, Jerry. *Four Reasons for the Elimination of Television*. New York: Morrow, 1977.

Marsden, George M. *Fundamentalism and American Culture*. New York: Oxford University Press, 1980.

Marty, Martin E. *A Nation of Behaviors*. Chicago: University of Chicago Press, 1976.

————. *Righteous Empire: The Protestant Experience in America*. New York: Dial, 1970.

Maslow, Abraham H. *Motivation and Personality*. New York: Harper and Row, 1970.

Mead, Margaret. *Culture and Commitment: The New Relations Between the Generations in the 1970s*. New York: Doubleday, 1978.

Mead, Sidney E. *Lively Experiment: The Shaping of Christianity in America*. New York: Harper and Row, 1963.

Meadows, D. H., and D. L. Meadows. *Limits to Growth*. New York: New American Library, 1974.

Mellis, Charles J. *Committed Communities: Fresh Streams for World Missions*. Pasadena: William Carey Library, 1976.

Menninger, Karl. *Whatever Became of Sin?* New York: Bantam, 1978.

Mooneyham, W. Stanley. *What Do You Say To A Hungry World*. Waco: Word, 1975.

Morgan, Marabel. *The Total Woman*. Old Tappan: Revell, 1976.

Morris, James. *Preachers*. New York: St. Martin's, 1973.

Mouw, Richard. *Called to Holy Worldliness*. Philadelphia: Fortress, 1980.

Mowrer, O. Hobart. *The New Group Therapy*. New York: Van Nostrand, 1964.

Niebuhr, H. Richard. *Christ and Culture*. New York: Harper and Row, 1951.

——. *The Kingdom of God in America*. New York: Harper and Row, 1937.

Nisbet, Robert. *History of the Idea of Progress*. New York: Basic, 1979.

Novak, Michael. *Rise of the Unmeltable Ethnics*. New York: Macmillan, 1972.

O'Connor, Elizabeth. *Journey Inward, Journey Outward*. New York: Harper and Row, 1975.

——. *The New Community*. New York: Harper and Row, 1976.

Olthuis, James H. *Facts, Values and Ethics*. Atlantic Highlands: Humanities, 1968.

Ortlund, Raymond C. *Lord, Make My Life a Miracle*. Glendale: Regal, 1974.

Perkins, John. *Let Justice Roll Down*. Glendale: Regal, 1976.

Phillips, J. B. *Your God Is Too Small*. New York: Macmillan, 1953.

——. *The New Testament in Modern English*. New York: Macmillan, 1958.

Poland, Larry. *Rise to Conquer: A Call for Committed Living*. Chappaqua: Christian Herald, 1979.

Quebedeaux, Richard. *The Worldly Evangelicals*. New York: Harper and Row, 1978.

——. *By What Authority: The Rise of Personality Cults in American Christianity*. New York: Harper and Row, 1982.

Ramm, Bernard L. *The Right, the Good, and the Happy*. Waco: Word, 1971.

Reich, Charles A. *The Greening of America: How the Youth Revolution Is Trying to Make America Liveable*. New York: Random House, 1970.

Richards, Lawrence O., and Clyde Hoeldtke. *A Theology of Church Leadership*. Grand Rapids: Zondervan, 1980.

Richey, Russell E. and Donald G. Jones, eds. *American Civil Religion*. New York: Harper and Row, 1974.

Ridenour, Fritz. *The Other Side of Morality*. Glendale: Regal, 1969.

Rifkin, Jeremy, and Ted Howard. *The Emerging Order: God in the Age of Scarcity*. New York: Putnam, 1979.

——. *Entropy: A New World View*. New York: Viking, 1980.

Rogers, Jack. *Biblical Authority*. Waco: Word, 1977.

Rose, Stephen C. *The Grass Roots Church*. New York: Holt, Rinehart and Winston, 1966.

Schaeffer, Francis A. *How Should We Then Live?* Old Tappan: Revell, 1976.

——. *Pollution and the Death of Man: The Christian View of Ecology*. Wheaton: Tyndale, 1970.

Schaller, Lyle. *The Change Agent: The Strategy of Innovative Leadership*. Nashville: Abingdon, 1972.

Schumacher, E. F. *A Guide for the Perplexed.* New York: Harper and Row, 1977.

_____. *Small is Beautiful: Economics as if People Mattered.* New York: Harper and Row, 1975.

Schur, Edwin M. *Awareness Trap: Self-Absorption Instead of Social Change.* New York: McGraw-Hill, 1977.

Sennett, Richard. *Fall of Public Man: The Social Psychology of Capitalism.* New York: Random House, 1978.

Selye, Hans. *Stress Without Distress.* New York: Harper and Row, 1974.

Sheehy, Gail. *Passages.* New York: Bantam, 1977.

_____. *Pathfinders.* New York: Morrow, 1981.

Sider, Ronald J. *Rich Christians in an Age of Hunger: A Biblical Study.* Downers Grove: InterVarsity, 1977.

Simon, Sidney B., et al. *Values Clarification.* New York: Hart, 1972.

Skinner, B. F. *Beyond Freedom and Dignity.* New York: Bantam, 1972.

_____. *Walden Two.* New York: Macmillan, 1948.

Slater, Philip E, and Warren G. Bennis. *The Temporary Society.* New York: Harper and Row, 1968.

Smart, James D. *The Cultural Subversion of the Biblical Faith.* Philadelphia: Westminster, 1977.

Snyder, Howard A. *The Community of the King.* Downers Grove: InterVarsity, 1977.

Solzhenitsyn, Alexander. *Warning to the West.* New York: Farrar, Straus, and Giroux, 1975.

Stewart, Edward C. *American Cultural Patterns: A Cross-Cultural Perspective.* LaGrange Park: Intercultural, 1972.

Stott, John C. *The Lausanne Covenant.* Minneapolis: World Wide Publications, 1975.

Streiker, Lowell D., and Gerald S. Strober. *Religion and the New Majority.* New York: Association, 1972.

Taylor, John V. *Enough Is Enough: A Biblical Call for Moderation in a Consumer Oriented Society.* Minneapolis: Augsburg, 1977.

Tippett, Alan R. *Solomon Islands Christianity: A Study in Growth and Obstruction.* Pasadena: William Carey Library, 1975.

Toffler, Alvin. *Future Shock.* New York: Random House, 1970.

_____. *The Third Wave.* New York: Morrow, 1980.

Tournier, Paul. *Guilt and Grace.* New York: Harper and Row, 1962.

_____. *The Meaning of Persons.* New York: Harper and Row, 1957.

Trueblood, Elton. *Company of the Committed.* New York: Harper and Row, 1980.

Tuchman, Barbara W. *A Distant Mirror: The Calamitous Fourteenth Century.* New York: Knopf, 1978.

Vanier, Vean. *Community and Growth.* New York: Paulist Press, 1979.

Wagner, C. Peter. *Your Spiritual Gifts Can Help Your Church Grow.* Glendale: Regal, 1979.

Wagner, C. Peter, and Edward R. Dayton. *Unreached Peoples.* Elgin: David C. Cook, 1979, 1980, 1981.

Wallis, Jim. *An Agenda for Biblical People.* New York: Harper and Row, 1976.

————. *The Call to Conversion.* New York: Harper and Row, 1981.

Webber, Robert. *Common Roots: A Call to Evangelical Maturity.* Grand Rapids: Zondervan, 1978.

————. *The Secular Saint: A Case For Evangelical Social Responsibility.* Grand Rapids: Zondervan, 1979.

Webber, Robert, and Donald Bloesch. *The Orthodox Evangelicals.* Nashville: Nelson, 1978.

Weber, Max. *Protestant Ethic and the Spirit of Capitalism.* Rev. ed. New York: Scribner, 1977.

White, John. *The Golden Cow.* Downers Grove: InterVarsity, 1979.

Wilson, Samuel, ed. *Mission Handbook.* Twelfth edition. Monrovia: MARC, 1981.

Yankelovich, Daniel. *New Rules: Searching for Self-Fulfillment in a World Turned Upside Down.* New York: Random House, 1981.

Yoder, John G. *The Politics of Jesus.* Grand Rapids: Eerdmans, 1972.

Scripture Index

Subject Index